More Praise for *Leaders as Teachers*

"There is a gigantic difference between great individual leaders and leaders who build great companies. It's one thing to make brilliant individual decisions, yet entirely another to cultivate a brilliant culture composed of wave upon wave of leaders who then teach generation upon generation of new leaders. When leaders master the art of teaching, they've laid a powerful foundation for an enduring great company."

Jim Collins
Author, *Good to Great*
Co-author, *Built to Last*

"Ed Betof has redefined a standard for excellence in leadership development! *Leaders as Teachers* establishes the business case and provides the guide for other organizations to release the untapped potential of their own leaders. In today's volatile business environment, using leaders as teachers is not just a good idea; it is a strategic business imperative."

Paul Erdahl
Vice President, Global Leadership & Talent Development
Medtronic

"A breakthrough way to improve your talent and business! This treasure trove of practices will enhance any leadership development effort by leveraging the resident skills and knowledge of your organization's leaders as they develop themselves and others. This book clearly demonstrates what I believe to be the most effective and efficient way to maximize talent investments! I would recommend this book to all senior executives seeking new ways to drive business results through teaching and learning initiatives."

Alan Todd
Chairman, Corporate University Xchange

"Betof's book makes a strong case for leaders as teachers. As a road map for success it is as good a GPS as I have seen."

Gordon Peters
Chairman and CEO, The Institute for Management Studies

"Leading for most managers does not come naturally. It must be learned, and who better to instill it than an organization's current leaders? Based on this wise premise, Ed Betof's *Leaders as Teachers* offers the comprehensive roadmap for building from within a complete and compelling leadership development program."

Michael Useem
Professor of Management and Director of the Center for Leadership and Change
Wharton School, University of Pennsylvania
Author, *The Leadership Moment*

"Ed Betof is a pioneer in promoting the concept of leaders as teachers. His strategies can revolutionize the way you think about and plan how to create a learning organization that is collaborative and dynamic. I strongly recommend this book to learning professionals and business executives, regardless of where they serve."

Mel Silberman
Author, *Active Training*
Editor, *The Handbook of Experiential Learning*

"The idea that we should leverage executives to help teach and train others in the organization has long been an important and sensible goal. *Leaders as Teachers* offers a hands-on guide for doing just that based on the transformation of one of our leading companies."

Peter Cappelli
George W. Taylor Professor of Management
Director, Center for Human Resources
Editor, *Academy of Management Perspectives*

"While it has been recognized that leaders' teaching and modeling skills will give tremendous credibility to training efforts there are many challenges to pulling it off in an organization. Ed Betof gives you a systematic, comprehensive approach to making this stick and becoming part of the fabric of your company."

Marty Seldman
Author, *Executive Stamina*

"Today's business environment requires organizations to develop their leaders and build a strong bench. Organizations whose leaders teach are best-in-class examples of what it takes to build a learning culture; engage employees; effectively communicate up, down, and across the company; and ultimately drive organizational success. Ed Betof and his team were pioneers in using leaders as teachers, were recognized by ASTD and other leading organizations for their success, and have written about it so that we can all learn from their experience. *Leaders as Teachers: Unlock the Teaching Potential of Your Company's Best and Brightest* is a must read for those with any interest in developing leaders at any level within an organization."

Tony Bingham
President and CEO, American Society for Training & Development

Leaders as Teachers

Unlock the Teaching Potential
of Your Company's
Best and Brightest

Leaders as Teachers

Unlock the Teaching Potential of Your Company's Best and Brightest

Edward Betof

ASTD
PRESS

Alexandria, Virginia

BK

Berrett–Koehler Publishers, Inc.
San Francisco
a BK Business book

ASTD Press is an internationally renowned source of insightful and practical information on workplace learning and performance topics, including training basics, evaluation and return on investment, instructional systems development, e-learning, leadership, and career development.

Ordering information: Books published by ASTD Press can be purchased by visiting our website at store.astd.org or by calling 800.628.2783 or 703.683.8100.

Library of Congress Control Number: 2008925909

ISBN-10: 1-56286-545-5
ISBN-13: 978-1-56286-545-0

ASTD Press Editorial Staff:
Director: Dean Smith
Manager, Acquisitions and Author Relations: Mark Morrow
Editorial Manager: Jacqueline Edlund-Braun
Senior Associate Editor: Tora Estep
Editorial Assistant: Georgina Del Priore

Copyeditor: Alfred Imhoff
Indexer: April Davis
Proofreader: Kris Patenaude
Interior Design and Production: Kathleen Schaner
Cover Design: Steve Fife
Cover Illustration: Shutterstock

Printed by United Book Press, Inc., Baltimore, Maryland

To my wife and life partner, Nila, with whom I have shared love and family and from whom I have learned for more than 40 years.

To my late Mom and Dad, Jean and Martin Betof, who taught me essential lessons throughout their lives and when I needed them the most.

To our son, Ari, our daughter, Allison, and our daughter-in-law, Shauna, whose goals, dreams, and zest for life will benefit so many others.

To my granddaughters, Anya Anne and Kayla Grace, who are blessed with parents and family who love them and who are helping them to become all they will choose to be.

To Ed Ludwig and the hundreds of leader-teachers throughout the world at BD as well as my BD University and talent management colleagues and teammates, who have fueled the leaders-as-teachers process since 2000.

Contents

Foreword

Leaders as Teachers: Unlock the Teaching Potential of Your Company's Best and Brightest is a book that any company serious about becoming great should embrace. This book invites executives and leaders into the classroom and will help them contribute to their company's growth in very important ways. The book can help business and functional leaders teach, facilitate, and coach others for real business results. For learning and development professionals, the book can serve as an in-depth implementation guide with hundreds of proven and practical suggestions. I am proud that BD's experience of becoming a benchmark company and effectively implementing the leaders-as-teachers approach on a global basis serves as part of the backdrop of the book.

I became president of BD (Becton, Dickinson and Company) in 1999, CEO in 2000, and chairman of the board in 2002. One of the first things I did as CEO was an organizational profile to find out from our associates what was getting in the way of BD becoming a great company. One of the things we learned was that not everyone knew where we were going. And we received a strong message that we had to spend more time developing people.

That strengthened my conviction that we had to extend and formalize our leadership and associate development process. Our ability to get to where we're going is powered by skillful, adaptable, engaged people.

We wanted more than traditional training—we'd been through many cycles of that, bringing in experts from schools like Harvard and Stanford once a year and moving from idea to idea. Further, in the absence of a strategically aligned process for training and development on a corporate-wide basis, our businesses around the globe were coming up with their own programs, and some of them were teaching management skills and behaviors that we felt were less than ideal. We wanted to promote the "BD Orthodoxy"—things BD believes to be true about the way we're running the company and what we expect from our leaders and associates.

To prepare for BD's next 100 years, we had to develop new skills, abilities, and approaches. And we believed that the best ways to do this was through a combination of challenging new roles, adding "stretch" to current assignments, including selected customized developmental assignments, a strong formalized curriculum, and leaders serving as teachers around the world. All this thinking led to the formation of BD University in 2000. In the years since 2000, our company's leaders-as-teachers approach has become an integral part of our business agenda. It has been vital to our leadership development efforts and has helped us continuously strengthen our culture and communications across the company. Our leaders-as-teachers approach was led by Ed Betof, our former vice president for talent management and chief learning officer. Our company has been honored with an ASTD Best Award in 2007, and the leaders-as-teachers approach has been the subject of numerous professional articles and presentations, and a best practices educational video.

Serving as a leader-teacher is very important to me, as it is to hundreds of other leaders in our company. Teaching gives me the opportunity to speak directly to people about where we are going, and about our journey to become a great company. Initially, teaching sessions made me understand that we needed to increase our communication substantially. I began to travel more; to make videos for employees; to hold conference calls; and to conduct town meetings to describe our purpose, our goals, our values, and our directions. I have taught in dozens of leadership programs and have also personally benefited in many ways. Teaching is one of the methods I use to try to stay in touch and to keep my finger on the pulse of the company. In my teaching role, I answer a lot of questions, and that's helped me clarify my own ideas about where the company should be going. I learn from teaching, and I think it has made me a better communicator of our strategies.

Frankly, I don't think the role of teacher is optional for a CEO in today's complex, multifunctional, multinational, technology-driven organizations. It's part of the job. And it's a fun part. I believe that the education in which we participate contributes to making the company grow faster, become more profitable, and achieve higher levels of customer satisfaction. It is also a vital complement to our associate engagement efforts.

When we recruit, we definitely want people to know that teaching will be part of their success at BD. They will be expected to take time to teach, coach, and develop people as well as to get into a formal training mode.

One of the things I'd like to be remembered for—and I hope this goes toward the top of the list—is that on my watch, the development of people became embedded in the organization's culture. I believe the maxim that a company's only sustainable competitive advantage is the ability to innovate, adapt, learn, and create new value for its customers. When leaders serve as teachers, this is all the more likely to occur. I am pleased that our ability to learn, teach, and grow has developed into an organizational flywheel. These efforts must keep going. If it does, we will have done something very important for the next generation.

I recommend *Leaders as Teachers* to your organization. It is a treasure trove for teaching and learning organizations.

Edward J. Ludwig
Chairman and Chief Executive Officer
Becton, Dickinson and Company
April 2009

Acknowledgments

I wish to extend my gratitude to the following individuals for their suggestions and encouragement in the preparation, review, and editing of this book:

Nila Betof, PhD, partner and chief operating officer of the Leaders Edge, whose ongoing support and ideas solidified my commitment to write this book.

Tora Estep, a senior associate editor with ASTD Press. Tora's final editing and management of the process from proofs through publication and distribution enabled the project to cross the finish line on time and in a high-quality manner. Her guidance in the final stages of the editing process has been invaluable to me.

Alfred Imhoff, who provided superb copy-editing that came just at the right time and helped me to complete the manuscript in a timely manner.

Jim Jerbasi, Jean-Marc Dageville, and Donna Boles to whom I reported in succession as they led the global BD human resources function since the late 1990s. Their support was instrumental in helping our efforts to establish the leaders-as-teachers approach and the creation and growth of BD University.

Donna McNamara, PhD, who implemented a very successful leaders-as-teachers process during her years as the leader of the learning function at the Colgate-Palmolive Company. Donna's feedback and ideas always proved useful as the manuscript evolved.

Mark Morrow, manager of acquisitions and author relations, ASTD Press, who provided invaluable support, encouragement, and editing throughout the writing project. Mark was available whenever I needed him, and I could not have completed this project without his input.

Cindy Scalice, training coordinator at BD, who assisted me in dozens of ways for more than five years in my role at the company and was ever responsive to answer questions and to help me locate documents and resources as I wrote the manuscript for this book.

Thomas Ruddy, PhD, who currently serves as vice president and leads the talent management and learning function at BD. Tom's support and timely review and approval of the manuscript allowed this project to be completed on time.

Joseph Toto, who has served as director of leadership development and learning at BD University beginning in 2002. Joe's partnership, teaching, and skill in advancing the leaders-as-teachers process around the world added immeasurably to the program's success. Joe provided ideas and edits throughout the writing process that have been incorporated as important points in this book.

Wendy Witterschein who has traveled the world as a key member of BD University's leadership team. Wendy has been a superb and creative role model in the recruitment, training, and preparation of leader-teachers across the globe. Wendy's insights, feedback, and ideas have added unique perspectives to this book.

Leaders as Teachers

Unlocking the Teaching Potential of Your Best and Brightest

Teaching is the highest form of understanding.
—Aristotle

*Setting an example is not the main means of influencing
another; it is the only means.*
—Albert Einstein

The concept of using an organization's leaders as a key component of a successful learning strategy might seem an obvious use of the many talented, dedicated leaders who work at all levels in every organization. Why not use the potential of these leaders to inspire, mentor, coach, and train other talented leaders, or even teams and team leaders, to enable them to reach their full potential? My goal in writing this book is to inspire those in other organizations to take this obvious leap and unlock the potential of leaders who are hungry to share their knowledge and experience with others.

In this book, I share what I have learned in my organization—BD (Becton, Dickinson and Company)—about how to design and implement strategically aligned and integrated leaders-as-teachers processes in business and organizational settings. The book is intended as both an informational guide and a practical implementation resource that will help you take this leap of faith and build your own leaders-as-teachers program. To accomplish this mission, I have provided a detailed road map that includes dozens of tips, hints, and implementation suggestions, along with useful worksheets, training agendas, and other support material. All the suggestions and ideas in this book are supported by practical experience and underpinned by sound theory that allows for application to a wide range of organizations.

Who Should Read This Book?

This book is primarily intended for learning and human resources leaders and professionals as well as business executives who wish to make teaching, coaching, and learning part of their formula for business and organizational success. Coaches who work with senior executives, including CEOs, will find this book a valuable resource. In addition, high-visibility leaders can use the concepts in this book to enhance their communication techniques.

Both a Strategic and Practical Guide

As noted, this book is both a strategic and practical implementation guide. Each chapter begins with a short introduction titled "What's Inside This Chapter." The chapters end with one or more implementation activities. The book accomplishes its strategic and practical goals by emphasizing

- the alignment of program selection and content development processes with business strategy and goals
- a careful selection and preparation of leader-teachers
- effective and active or experiential teaching by leaders
- active participant learning with a high potential for application and impact
- implementation based on personal learning experiences that contribute to business, organizational, team, and individual success.

Origins of BD's Success Story

BD's journey to a successful leaders-as-teachers program began in early 2000 when it took the first steps to establish BD University (BDU). Since then, more than 500 leaders have taught and served as the primary faculty for BDU. More than 90 percent of the classroom teaching at BDU is done by BD leader-teachers, including BD's chairman and chief executive officer, Edward J. Ludwig. As the senior executive of the company, Ed's ability and willingness to be actively engaged as a leader-teacher have set the example and a high standard for others in the organization. He regularly teaches in BD's Leadership and Advanced Leadership Development programs, which are offered in many parts of the world. On those infrequent occasions when he cannot be physically present, without missing a beat, he has taught and conducted town meetings using videoconferencing and teleconferencing technologies. He is also a guest speaker in other programs and is a knowledge sharer and communicator by nature and by training.

The Results Are Evident

The leaders-as-teachers approach has contributed in a variety of ways to BD's growth and its journey toward becoming a great company. During the eight years since the launch of BDU, BD has experienced strong and steady financial growth, outperformed many firms in its peer group, and more than doubled its worldwide sales and profitability. It has also been formally recognized as a great place to work by *Fortune* magazine and has been selected as an employer of choice in a number of states and countries. Through its science, technology, business practices, volunteerism, and philanthropy, BD continues to pursue its "Three Greats": great performance, great contributions to society, and being a great place to work. In addition to its many other business, philanthropic, social, and ethical accomplishments, BD has become a "best-in-class" example of how to deploy leaders and selected professionals as teachers. This approach to teaching and learning has become the foundation and "brand" of BDU.

The success of BD's program has inspired other organizations as well. Employees of other companies regularly visit BD to benchmark BD's leaders-as-teachers approach and practices. And BD's efforts have been recognized by professional workplace learning and development societies as well as research and consulting groups such as ASTD, the Corporate University Exchange, Accenture Learning, and the Center for Creative Leadership. BD's success story has also been told in numerous articles, staff presentations at professional conferences, and even a professional video documentary that tells BD's leaders-as-teachers story.

BD's leaders-as-teachers story is an important one. But in this book, it is simply a backdrop to enable the reader to gain a better understanding of the leaders-as-teachers approach. It is a paradigm of organizational practice from which other organizations can learn and which they can subsequently customize as they seek to develop what will work best in their context and culture. This book's approach can add tremendous value to a very wide range of organizations, yet it is culturally adaptable for each setting.

The Book's Design and Organization

This book's design enables you to easily read and use it as a whole or to read just the content that applies to your particular situation. Alternatively, each of the nine chapters, and even parts of these chapters, can be used separately to meet specific performance or learning needs. Throughout the book, I try not only to communicate what I have learned but also to present it in such a way so that you can tailor the leaders-as-teachers approach to your organization on either a smaller or larger scale. For example, when implementing the ideas in this book, you could start with one or two small efforts where leaders teach. You might conclude that you wish to keep your organizational approach relatively small. You could also design your approach for significantly larger yet measured and incremental growth. Regardless of the size and scope, this book explains the "whats," the "whys," and the "hows" to help you get off to a great start and then to sustain your progress.

The book is organized in eight chapters in addition to this chapter. Here is a brief description of each chapter.

Chapter 2: Why the Leaders-as-Teachers Approach Works— Six Strategic Organizational Benefits

Chapter 2 describes how the leaders-as-teachers approach supports an organization's business agenda. It includes a short case study of BD's implementation experience. You will also find an in-depth examination of the six key business benefits of using the leaders-as-teachers approach, which include

1. Helps drive business results
2. Stimulates the learning and development of leaders and associates
3. Improves the leadership skills of those who teach
4. Strengthens the organizational culture and communications
5. Promotes positive business and organizational change
6. Reduces costs by leveraging top talent.

In addition to providing the strategic rationale for the decision to adopt a leaders-as-teachers approach, this chapter sets the stage for the remainder of the book, which focuses on how to launch a leaders-as-teachers program in your organization.

Chapter 3: A Role for Every Leader—Dozens of Ways Leaders Can Teach

Chapter 3 is organized around the five broad categories or approaches by which leaders teach, coach, and contribute to learning and training programs and, more broadly, to organizational learning. More than 50 specific leader-teacher methods are described. These methods are grouped and presented thematically in five broad categories:

1. Identification of learning needs and design of learning solutions and programs
2. Live teaching
3. Teaching through the use of media and technology
4. Preprogram and postprogram teaching and coaching to help ensure application and impact of learning
5. Recruiting, training, coaching, and mentoring leader-teachers.

Chapter 4: Yes, Where You Work! Why Leaders Want to Teach and Come Back for More

Chapter 4 describes how to attract, engage, and retain leaders to serve as teachers and explores why these leaders want to serve. Drawing on principles and concepts of the leadership, career, and organizational experts Bernard

Haldane, Noel Tichy, and Tim Butler and Jim Waldroop, the book presents an integrated motivational model that reveals how to tap the energy, talent, and deeply embedded life interests that can be found in all organizations to drive your efforts to introduce a leaders-as-teachers approach.

Chapter 5: Defying Gravity—Orchestrating a Leaders-as-Teachers Change Process

Chapter 5 further describes the critical change process that must be addressed in a leaders-as-teachers approach. Change and leadership concepts derived from Jim Collins, John Kotter, and other leading thinkers can be invaluable for implementing a leaders-as-teachers approach. This chapter explores the essential elements of leading change and *how* you can use these elements to champion the implementation of a leaders-as-teachers process. The importance of senior leader and high-influencer involvement, not just support, is emphasized. Examples from BD's experiences support the principles and serve as a model for implementation in your organization.

Chapter 6: Help Your Leaders Be Stars—The Four Principles for Recruiting and Preparing Leaders to Teach

Recruiting and preparation are two of the keys to a successful program. Chapter 6 focuses on how to recruit leader-teachers and how to help them become stars. You will find many practical examples of techniques. Organized around four overarching principles or truths about leader-teacher recruitment and preparation, this chapter emphasizes the importance of

- ♦ Matching leaders' background, expertise, responsibilities, and teaching interests with program content and teaching assignments
- ♦ Teaching confidence based on preparation
- ♦ Teaching readiness
- ♦ Using active teaching and training methods in program design.

Chapter 7: Make Learning Content Come Alive—Helping Leaders Spark Active Learning Experiences

Learning content, structure, and approach are essential to helping leaders spark an active and meaningful learning experience. Chapter 7 describes active teaching and active learning methodologies and provides practical answers to common questions about this approach to learning. In addition, a baker's dozen of active teaching methods for leaders as teachers is offered. These multipurpose teaching and facilitation methods can be adapted and used for many content areas and programs and are applicable for many cultural settings around the world. To help you design your program, the Three-Level Program Design Model is offered and a case example is provided. This model is a practical framework for actively involving program participants in their own learning. The model can also be used to increase learning retention and encourage follow-through and application by the learner.

Chapter 8: Marine Boot Camp Tight: Answering Nine Key Questions to Ensure Successful Operations

Every successful program needs a solid administrative and operational framework and the infrastructure mechanisms and processes to efficiently support a leaders-as-teachers approach. Chapter 8 helps you create a hassle-free administrative environment by exploring these topics:

- How does governance affect the leaders-as-teachers process?
- What role do learning professionals play in the success of the leaders-as-teachers approach?
- How are the logistics of programs best handled?
- Why is advanced and reliable scheduling important?
- Why is it important to contract with leader-teachers for the session they have agreed to teach?
- What are the factors to consider when matching instructor teams?
- Program champions have a unique role. How do they help the leaders-as-teachers approach?

◆ What is the role of scorecards, dashboards, and "State of the Union" reports?

◆ How can you best manage vendor selection and relationships?

Chapter 9: Wrapping Up and Getting Started

The capstone of chapter 9 is the implementation activity titled "Your 12-Month Road Map—Implementing the Leaders-as-Teachers Approach in Your Organization." Though the chapter sums up the previous chapters, it also offers implementation signposts in the form of "Twelve Quick Reminders to Keep You on Track" and a useful recap of the questions presented in this book about the key issues that have challenged leaders and colleagues pursuing teachers-as-leaders programs, including

1. What are the reasons for a company to implement a leaders-as-teachers approach?

2. What are the different ways in which leaders can teach and contribute to individual and organizational learning?

3. How do we get our senior leaders and other leaders on board?

4. What is the best way to recruit leader-teachers?

5. What is the best way to prepare leaders to teach?

6. How can program and curriculum design help leaders become effective and exciting teachers?

7. How do we get started, and what should be our first steps? How do we build momentum once we get started?

8. Should leader-teachers be "certified" to teach?

9. Should we "decertify" leaders if they are ineffective teachers, and if so, how do we do it?

10. How can an organization's administrative and operating processes as well as infrastructure best support the leaders-as-teachers process?

Sources

The references cited and sources used in writing the book, along with additional resources, are listed at the end of the book.

See Leaders as Teachers in Action

If you would like to see firsthand how a leaders-as-teachers program works and feel the excitement it brings to organizational learning, go to www.astd .org/leadersasteachers or to www.corpu.com/leadersasteachers, where you will find a link to *The People Factor: Leaders as Teachers at BD*, a 23-minute film produced by the Corporate University Exchange that vividly describes the leaders-as-teachers process at BD.

Why the Leaders-as-Teachers Approach Works

Six Strategic Organizational Benefits

Leadership and learning are indispensable to each other.
—John F. Kennedy

The best time to plant a tree was twenty years ago.
The second best time is now.
—Chinese proverb

◆ ◆ ◆

What's Inside This Chapter?

This chapter describes how the leaders-as-teachers approach supports an organization's business agenda. It includes a short case study of BD's implementation experience and an in-depth examination of the six key business benefits of using a leaders-as-teachers approach as part of your corporate learning strategy. These business benefits include

- ◆ Helps drive business results
- ◆ Stimulates the learning and development of leaders and associates
- ◆ Improves the leadership skills of those who teach
- ◆ Strengthens the organizational culture and communications

- ◆ Promotes positive business and organizational change
- ◆ Reduces costs by leveraging top talent.

In addition to providing the strategic rationale behind a decision to adopt a leaders-as-teachers approach, this chapter sets the stage for the remainder of the book, which focuses on how to launch a leaders-as-teachers program in your organization.

The chapter concludes with the first of the book's frequently asked questions: What value does the leaders-as-teachers approach add to organizations? The first implementation activity is also included.

◆ ◆ ◆

Launching Leaders as Teachers

In late 1999, BD's senior leaders were faced with an intriguing puzzle. How could the company achieve its aggressive growth goals when it was clear that staying the course in terms of organizational learning was not a viable option? BD needed to do something bold. After considerable study and deliberation, BD made a commitment to pursue the goal of becoming a teaching organization *and* a learning organization. The idea of "leaders as teachers" became the backbone of BD University. Though the study team and, subsequently, BD's executive team embraced this idea, the consensus view was that implementation would be challenging. (See below for the details.)

◆ ◆ ◆

BD (Becton, Dickinson and Company): A Leaders-as-Teachers Case Study

In 2000, BD celebrated its 103rd birthday. The year began with BD's new CEO, Edward J. Ludwig, assuming office in a carefully planned succession. BD is a proud medical technology company steeped in a rich history of progressive business growth and generous corporate citizenship and with a strong values system whose associates typically stay for a long time. Yet the company was facing difficult, uncertain times.

Like many other companies, BD found itself competing in an external environment that looked very different from the global health care world that it had helped to shape during the previous century. Markets and regulations were changing quickly, as were customer buying patterns. The historically strong BD brands were only able to partly fuel its expected growth. Such was the challenge faced by Ed Ludwig and his BD Leadership Team.

There was much work to be done at BD. But its employees' dedication and work ethic never waned. Nor did BD's strong values system. During the 1990s, a worldwide corporate process distilled BD's rich past and projected future into four key values:

◆ We accept personal responsibility.
◆ We treat each other with respect.
◆ We always seek to improve.
◆ We do what is right.

As BD moved through 2000, the good news was that its committed, creative associates and leaders were the building blocks for entering the new century. However, a company's habits and history may simultaneously be its blessings and its curse by making things too familiar and usually easier. There is an expression that "gravity never has a bad day." Left unchecked, organizational habits will gravitate to a comfortable steady state that rarely leads to excellence. But these habits are also very hard to change.

The new century would call for BD leaders and associates to use the best of their past ways of working—their existing habits—while forming new and better ways to get things done. As a company, BD would need to challenge itself to change significantly.

With this realization, a clear vision and a new leadership platform for the next decade became paramount. New products and marketing platforms had to be developed and successfully launched. Manufacturing and transactional work processes would need to become much more efficient, lean, and capable of continuous improvement. New skills, knowledge, much greater speed, and personal and organizational agility had become essential. In some cases, the company was ready; in others, it was not.

Two examples illustrate the challenge BD faced in 2000:

◆ BD pioneered the use of a new generation of medical devices designed to significantly decrease both patient and health care workers' risks of injury and disease when using injectable products and surgical sharps. *Educating and training key parts of*

13

> *the workforce as well as customers on these new safety-based devices became paramount for this game-changing strategy to be successful.*

◆ BD discovered, developed, and brought to market a generation of diagnostic instruments, devices, and reagents that serve the fields of infectious disease, immunology, endocrinology, and oncology. Essentially, BD was now involved in breakthrough or potentially breakthrough technologies in all three of its worldwide business segments. *The related knowledge and skill sets in functional areas as diverse as molecular biology, microbiology, engineering, information technology, process development, engineering, marketing, sales, law, and human resources all need further development.*

Successful advances in medical devices, human diagnostics, the biotechnologies, and the life sciences are dependent on many factors. But there is one common denominator for all BD's growth initiatives: advancing the capabilities of BD associates and leaders to new levels of readiness.

The company realized that its growth strategies and the many other challenges it faced would require its associates at all levels—from the factory floor to senior leaders—to develop new skills, abilities, and talents to be able to take it in these new and different directions. *Most important, it was recognized that BD would need better, more consistently effective leadership.* The company's approaches to talent management were not adequate. Performance management, recruiting, total compensation, new leader assimilation, and, clearly, learning and development processes all needed improvement, rebuilding, and even reinventing.

From a historical perspective of learning and training, BD had a number of fine examples of programs over the years. But BD had inconsistent learning and training practices that frequently lacked sustainability and were often subject to the ebbs and flows of annual business performance. The organization did not share effective programs or approaches across business or geographic boundaries. This problem had organizational, structural, and cultural roots. By 2000, there were very few tangible remains of the learning and training investments made over the years. Certainly learning and development did not constitute an effective and institutionalized part of BD. It was not a core competence, and it could not be consistently leveraged for business growth (adapted from Betof 2004).

Faced with these tremendous challenges and opportunities, in 2000 Ed Ludwig and the BD Leadership Team formulated the concept of BD's "Journey to Become a Great Company" and the "Three Greats." Today, every BD associate—from Europe to Japan, from Singapore to Brazil, from Mexico City to corporate headquarters in Franklin Lakes, New Jersey— understands BD's definition of what constitutes a great company:

♦ great performance
♦ great contributions to society
♦ a great place to work.

Another key piece of BD's blueprint for the future involved the formulation of BD's three growth strategies:

1. Accelerate top-line growth through innovation and the development of higher-value products for the patients and the customers we serve.
2. Improve bottom-line growth by improving operational effectiveness.
3. Strengthen organizational, leadership, and associate capabilities.

BD's values, the "Three Greats," and BD's three growth strategies are core building blocks for the future. Together with the company's committed purpose, "Helping All People to Live Healthy Lives," these building blocks have become BD's fundamental blueprint for growth as a company. Since 2000, they have been the company's platform, path, and vision for its future.

Today, BD is a much stronger company. Sales are at record highs. Profitability is strong. Work processes have been measurably improved, and BD has an enterprise-wide integrated information data system that is both customer and company focused.

♦ ♦ ♦

Like many bold ideas developed in complex organizations, the road to implementation of the leaders-as-teachers idea began with extensive dialogue—in fact, 45 days of intense benchmarking, analysis, and discussion. At the end of this intense period of dialogue among key stakeholders, Ed Ludwig—BD's chairman and CEO—and his executive team approved a new learning strategy that relied on live, face-to-face learning with BD leaders and associates teaching other BD leaders and associates—that is, leaders as teachers. This idea was enthusiastically embraced by BD's leaders.

From the beginning, Ed participated as an active leader-teacher and taught in dozens of leadership programs, including the first offered by BD University (BDU) for senior leaders in the spring of 2000. From the beginning, he truly believed in the power of the leaders-as-teachers approach and supported the effort with visionary zeal. He embraced the leaders-as-teachers approach and saw it as a powerful catalyst for growth and change at BD. His active participation sent an important signal to other BD leaders and the entire organization.

Although the leaders-as-teachers initiative was a bold move, the organization's leaders understood that they were not venturing into completely uncharted waters. In fact, Noel Tichy—the author of numerous books and articles on leadership, including *The Leadership Engine* (1997) and the *The Cycle of Leadership* (2002)—wrote in 1998:

> We have looked at winning companies—those that consistently outperform competitors and reward shareholders and found that they've moved beyond being learning organizations to become teaching organizations.... That's because teaching organizations are more agile, come up with better strategies, and are able to implement them more effectively....
>
> Teaching organizations do share with learning organizations the goal that everyone continually acquires new knowledge and skills. But to do that they add the more critical goal that everyone pass their learning on to others.

Leader's Perspective

Edward J. Ludwig (chairman and CEO, BD) says: Teaching gives me the opportunity to talk directly to people about where we are going and about our journey to become a great company. Initially, these sessions made me understand that we needed to increase our communication substantially. I began to travel more; to make videos for employees; to hold conference calls; and to send email about our purpose, our goals, our values, and our directions.

In teaching organizations, leaders see it as their responsibility to teach. They do that because they understand that it's the best, if not only, way to develop throughout a company people who can come up with and carry out smart ideas about the business…. In teaching organizations, leaders benefit just by preparing to teach others. Because the teachers are people with hands-on experience within the organization—rather than outside consultants—the people being taught learn relevant, immediately useful concepts and skills….

Teaching organizations are better able to achieve success and maintain it because their constant focus is on developing people to become leaders (Tichy and Cohen 1998, 2–3).

BD University: A Successful Record

Once BD's leaders signed onto the program, it was only a few months until the first live BDU leader-led programs were conducted. By 2004, much of the required curriculum, consisting of six courses for all people and team managers and leaders, had been deployed globally. By the beginning of 2008, thousands of implementation plans or committed actions that resulted from learning and developmental experiences in BDU programs had been put to the test in actual work situations. Since the program's launch, more than 500 BD leaders have been certified as leader-teachers, and 50,000 BDU "participant seats" have been filled. Leaders have taught at venues around the world in one or more of several dozen BDU programs in BD's Leadership College, Business Skills College, Operational Effectiveness College, Career Development College, and Sales College.

Today, essentially all members of the BD Leadership Team teach in all or parts of one or more BDU programs. In addition, many other leaders and associates teach in programs, or in less formal settings that are not actually part of BDU, such as those with high technical, scientific, or strong, functionally specific content.

> **Leader's Perspective**
> Vince Forlenza (executive vice president, BD) says: I found teaching another way to connect to my organization, particularly to individuals I did not work with every day. It gave me the opportunity to hear their issues firsthand and share my thoughts directly. I formed new relationships that helped manage the business. Teaching often gave me the opportunity to challenge the organization while giving them the tools to solve problems. It is not just the students who grow during the course but the teachers as well. Teaching has been an important part of my own leadership development.

Curriculum Supported by Technology

Every aspect of the BDU curriculum is designed to support business goals, strategies, and growth. BDU began primarily with live classroom teaching and learning. But as its program grew, BD leaders and associates added technology-enabled and blended learning and performance support solutions. Some were as simple as technologically available executive book summaries that could be read individually or discussed in teams or in classes. Other technology-enabled resources support sales, new product development, manufacturing, regulatory affairs, compliance, and the supply chain as well as management leadership roles. (This topic is discussed in greater detail in chapter 3.)

Real Benefits

Today, nearly nine years after its founding, other companies frequently visit the BDU team and benchmark its leaders-as-teachers approach and practices. In addition, professional learning and development societies and respected benchmarking, research, and leadership development organizations—such as ASTD, the Corporate University Exchange, Accenture Learning, and the Center for Creative Leadership—have recognized BD's efforts through awards, documentaries, articles, and invitations to speak about BDU's success. (See the sidebar for a more detailed history of BDU's development.)

Since 2000, BD's revenue and profit base has more than doubled and continues to grow throughout the world. It has met or exceeded its own and analysts' expectations for more than 30 consecutive quarters. Several times, the company has been named as one of America's most admired companies by *Fortune* magazine. In 2007, BD was also named to the inaugural list of world's most ethical companies by *Ethisphere Magazine*. The company was selected that year for the second time as a component of the Dow Jones Sustainability World Index, which is recognized as the premier socially responsible investing index. ASTD recognized BD and its leaders-as-teachers approach in 2007 by giving the firm a BEST Award. During this same period, a major shift occurred in the number of leaders who think of themselves as *leader-coaches* and who make coaching and teaching part of their everyday responsibilities.

◆ ◆ ◆

How BDU Supports Leaders as Teachers

Leaders as teachers extends the reach of the seven-person BDU staff by 30 to 35 Global Core Team members. These are BD associates who, in addition to their regular jobs as business and functional professionals and leaders, conduct ongoing needs analyses, select initiatives and develop solutions, and staff small subteams to continuously improve BD University and leaders-as-teachers service delivery. The entire group of about 40 meets by teleconference every six weeks and in person at a worldwide conference every one to two years (*T&D* 2007).

The BDU Global Core Team also ensures regular "swapping and sharing" or "importing and exporting" of both program and process ideas and materials seamlessly across geographic borders. This normative behavior contributes to high levels of organizational learning and knowledge transfer throughout BD. A very significant advantage of the leaders-as-teachers approach is the forging of internal networks that are accessed regularly, become peer support mechanisms, and aid in getting everyday work done.

Members of the BDU Global Core Team also teach. These leader-teachers, as well as the hundreds of others from around the world, regularly report on the personal benefits they gain from their teaching efforts: "In addition to the strategic learning and development managed by BDU, hundreds of hours of product and technical training are delivered throughout the 50-country, matrixed-structured organization, in which nearly two-thirds of employees work in manufacturing locations. Businesses, regions, and functions can, and do, develop their own programs based on market and associates' needs" (*T&D* 2007, 40). These are regularly shared with other parts of the organization once they become established in the originating site.

◆ ◆ ◆

Six Reasons to Implement a Leaders-as-Teachers Approach

Since BD has focused its energies on developing the potential of leaders as teachers, the organization has benefited in many ways. The program has helped to drive and support business results and has helped enable cost reductions by aligning business and learning strategies and by strengthening associates' capabilities. It has promoted positive business and organizational change. It has improved BD's organizational culture and strengthened its communications. It has also improved the leadership skills of both the leaders teaching and their students. These benefits can be analyzed in terms of six reasons to implement a leaders-as-teachers approach.

Helping to Drive Business Results

The first reason to implement a leaders-as-teachers approach is that it drives business results by ensuring strategic business alignment between senior business leaders and the programs and services provided by the learning function. In today's business environment, all learning programs and resources should support business strategy and goals. They must, in some way, support organizational, team, or individual performance or performance improvement. Typically, a corporate university or learning function aligns program content with business and organizational strategy by working with company executives to design a highly interactive governance process and structure.

Generally, these senior and high-potential leaders work with the leaders of the learning function to oversee the learning curricula and provide strategic business perspectives during a collaborative planning process. Ultimately, the organization as a whole benefits tremendously from this close working relationship. Under the corporate university model, for example, a very senior executive might serve as the dean of the corporate university and partner directly with the chief learning officer as part of his or her broader executive responsibilities. Several executives might serve as deans or directors of specific colleges or institutes within the corporate university. Or a small group of executives might serve as an advisory board for the chief learning officer and the learning team. The organization's choice of structure is important in that it enables healthy

---

Leader's Perspective

Gary Cohen (executive vice president, BD) says: I have had the opportunity to participate in multiple sessions of BD's Leadership Development Program and Advanced Leadership Development Program as a teacher. I can personally attest that the participants gain significantly from having senior leaders in the company participate as teachers. Among the benefits to the participants are the opportunity to get to know their leaders in a more personal way, the ability to learn how leadership development principles can be applied in a manner consistent with the company's culture, and the gaining of insight regarding the company's current priorities and future plans. I would also say that an even more meaningful benefit is that when leaders participate as teachers and join our leadership development courses for a full three days, it makes the participants feel important and appreciated. Many are surprised that our highest-level (and often busiest) executives would literally stop their other activities to devote so much time to associate development. Personally, I have also gained from these sessions, in large part based on the opportunity to get to know many of our associates in a deeper manner than would occur in the normal business environment. It also enabled me to gain insight into people who might have significant future leadership potential and provided a means to sense the "pulse" of the organization at the time the development sessions were being held. The company benefits in many ways, not the least of which is the opportunity to "humanize" our senior leaders and establish a more direct connection among people at different levels of the organization. The company also greatly benefits from the direct transference of knowledge and insight regarding the company's culture and business priorities. In addition, this approach allows for an educational experience that is highly pertinent and directly based on the goals the organization is working to achieve. It clearly overcomes the tendency for classroom style instruction to be theoretical rather than practical.

and proactive interplay between the company's key executives and its learning leaders. This helps ensure strategic business alignment and interaction among the business's leaders, its learning function, and its programs and services.

New Level of Senior-Level Involvement

A leaders-as-teachers program strengthens this relationship and in fact serves as a type of organizational insurance policy for leaders who teach. Leaders are confident that the content they teach and the sessions they facilitate are vetted by senior and other leaders who are part of the teaching-learning process. Moreover, the leaders know that the overall curricula and specific program content they teach reflects the most current and anticipated business realities and culture of the organization.

Other Alignment

General managers, functional directors and vice presidents, and geographic leaders such as regional or divisional presidents, vice presidents, or directors typically have the responsibility to create business plans, set key priorities, and deliver on those plans. Teaching offers the opportunity to communicate and engage others in these plans. Leaders can communicate their reasoning for decisions and assumptions for success. In the right environment, these interactions are highly conducive to productive dialogue and reality testing.

Leaders who participate as subject matter experts in the program development process also enhance this strategic alignment benefit by ensuring that key strategic, business, and functional points of view are incorporated into the development of important programs. Let's look at an example based on my BD experience.

Focused Interviews Are Keys to Success

Joe Toto and I were charged with developing BD's high-profile Advanced Leadership Development Program, in which more than 1,000 BD leaders have participated since 2004. Early in the design process, Joe and I decided that it was essential to directly involve the top half-dozen executives at BD. Over the course of about six to nine months, we interviewed these executives three times. In the first cycle, in individual interviews that Joe and I conducted together, we asked these executives to react to the basic design concepts and primary content themes. We took the executive input and that of others and worked on the next version of the program design. When we felt we had a valuable and credible draft design, we scheduled a second round of interviews. These interviews were very encouraging and confirmed that we were on the right path. Once again, we took the feedback and suggestions and further developed the program design. About two months later, we did the third and final round of interviews. The information we gained from these interviews enabled us to do the necessary fine-tuning to finalize the program launch design.

It is important to emphasize that our meetings with these executives centered on specific concepts and content set up for reaction and feedback. At the end of each interview, we committed to returning with the next stage of the design. This iterative process directly engaged the executives and ensured commitment. These meetings built on the positive experience that each executive had as an active participant in the creation of the first BDU flagship leadership programs, the Leadership Development Program. In addition, each executive had become a teaching role model in this program and now had committed to launching the Advanced Leadership Development Program. These senior leader-teachers truly put skin in the game.

Another Strategic Alignment Example

Leaders participating in program design is another example of business results–driven strategic alignment. In this case, the senior executive accountable for globally strengthening BD's manufacturing and operational excellence processes (part of BD's core growth strategies since 2000) concluded that the company's strategy needed to be supported by a highly visible leadership development program focused entirely on this vital area. The resulting BD Leading Operational Effectiveness Program, designed in 2002 and early 2003 with the full involvement of BD's global process leaders, is an excellent example of how this collaborative process can drive business results. The course is regularly updated consistent with continuous improvement changes in the company's supply chain, manufacturing, and operational processes. The program has been taught four times a year by BD's global process leaders since its launch in 2003 and, more important, it has served as a catalyst for clarifying important unresolved concepts and process issues that have a direct impact on operational effectiveness.

Aligning Program Content and Organization Strategy

Here is another way that both leader-teachers and subject matter experts can also help align program content with company strategy, business results, and building desired organizational culture. Approximately six weeks before a new program is launched, a carefully selected group of BD leader-teachers, subject matter experts, and members of BDU's learning team convene. Usually about six to 12 leaders and professionals participate in this process known as a program shakedown. This unique prelaunch quality control process begins with a half-day session facilitated by the new program champion, who presents the content, and the instructional-facilitator design is reviewed and critiqued. The process helps ensure alignment with strategic, business, and cultural goals and standards, as well as vetting content and instructional soundness. Most important, leader-teachers who will teach in the initial program sessions are also invited to participate in this shakedown session.

◆ ◆ ◆

Other Ways Leader-Teachers Add Business Value

Here are two other ways that leader-teachers help to ensure business strategic alignment and integration in the learning process. The first is town meetings as part of learning programs that present key company issues and field participants' questions related to strategy and real-time issues. This is an excellent way for leaders to teach and to focus on essential business, strategic, and organizational issues. Conducting town meetings generally does not require a tremendous amount of preparation unless very sensitive or potentially volatile issues need to be addressed. An easy format for town meetings is for a leader to start the meeting with five to 10 minutes of opening comments followed by approximately 45 minutes of questions and answers.

The second way that leader-teachers help to ensure business strategic alignment and integration in the learning process is guest speaking and coteaching. For example, one of BD's four basic values is *We always do what is right*. In the company's Ethical Fitness Program and in several of its other leadership development programs, the principle of *Setting the tone at the top* is regularly taught. These topics can be incorporated into other programs and presented by appropriate leader-teachers.

Leaders who teach engage with others in the classroom in ways that allow them to sense the organization as well as solicit and receive information to which they would not otherwise have access. This helps them calibrate their strategies and test out their own leadership thinking and effectiveness. I have regularly heard leaders say that they found the interchange with a class they taught, with the members of a town meeting they conducted, or with the audience when they have been a guest speaker to be very valuable. They are able to participate in commentary that provides them with information they did not previously have. They are able to test run ideas. The informality of the classroom allows for the type of healthy dialogue that often does not exist in day-to-day work settings. All this communication and interaction help leaders perform at high levels and continuously improve their strategic, business, and talent management responsibilities and capabilities.

◆ ◆ ◆

Informal Interaction and Conversation

Finally, company strategy, priorities, and leadership points of view are often clarified, reinforced, and, sometimes, privately debated among fellow leader-teachers when they coteach. For example, offline discussions that occur when students are working on tasks, group activities, during meals, or at session breaks sometimes bring valuable strategic insight. Some of the most important discussions I have had with other leaders about company strategy and hot organizational topics have occurred as a result of these informal conversations. This is a subtle but important strategic alignment and integration dynamic that occurs when leaders coteach. This dynamic has an important effect in building deeper understanding among leaders.

Stimulating the Learning and Development of Leaders and Associates

The second reason to implement a leaders-as-teachers approach is that it serves as a catalyst for the learning and development of the leaders and associates who participate as students in leader-led programs. This dynamic occurs in three ways: role modeling, creating a safe environment for feedback, and building networks.

Role Modeling

One of the most meaningful ways learners experience what is really important in the organization is through role modeling by their leaders. Imagine your CEO, presidents of global or national businesses, and functional leaders teaching principles of leadership or company strategy. What if a broad range of leaders were facilitating classes on diversity and inclusion, coaching, and selecting the best? Or what if your financial leaders in many countries were teaching a program on finance for nonfinancial managers? Or what if your manufacturing and continuous improvement process leaders were also the teachers and facilitators of programs designed to drive quality and productivity in those areas? The impressions made and lessons learned in teaching-learning scenarios like these are very important. Call it matching word and deed or walking the talk. Program participants who work in companies where leaders teach have a high likelihood of understanding what is regarded as important as well as what is valued and important and what is not. They have the benefit of having positive role models in and outside of the classroom.

Creating a Safe Environment for Feedback

Learners have opportunities to practice skills and behaviors in safe environments and get feedback from leader-teachers and peers before trying to implement them in their real work settings. In learning situations like this, participants have opportunities to hear from, have ideas sparked, and interact with leaders other than those with whom they typically work.

There are many advantages when leaders teach institutional knowledge, cultural expectations, and skills expected of managers, leaders, and associates. When these are practiced in the classroom, learners are able to try out the uncomfortable and hear perspectives and receive feedback from leaders to whom they typically do not report. This provides degrees of realism and safety. Ideas can be tested. Skills can be practiced. When leaders teach in these situations, they are able to provide points of views and observations that have inherent value often more so than what professional trainers can add by themselves. The combination of leader-teachers who cotrain with learning and development professionals may provide the best of both worlds for students. In these types of environments, learners have an opportunity to test their ideas and creatively explore possible solutions to the problems and challenges they face with leader-teachers and learning professionals who can serve as short-term coaches and advisers in and outside the classroom.

Building Networks

Learners have an opportunity to build important networks with leaders who can be resources for helping them to perform their roles more effectively once the class has ended. Postclass interaction and follow-up between students and leaders who teach are not uncommon. This is an additional way of fostering the type of coaching culture that so many organizations seek. In similar ways, learners have opportunities to build important networks with leaders who can be resources for expanding their career options and opportunities. Learners also have opportunities to make positive impressions on those leaders who teach and who also are heavily involved in talent and succession planning for their respective teams and organizations. Conversely, leader-teachers have opportunities to be "talent scouts" while teaching those whom they know as well as other learners whom they may not have previously met. This can lead to career and developmental opportunities that would not otherwise occur.

Reverse Talent Scouts

Learners also have opportunities to do "reverse talent scouting" of leader-teachers whom they might later ask to become mentors or, when the timing is right, for whom they might seek opportunities for new roles in their respective teams or organizations. This type of multidirectional talent scouting can be a very healthy dynamic in an age of employee "free agency" and at a time when employees are increasingly being asked to assume primary responsibility for their career development.

When leaders teach, learners also gain a different kind of developmental experience by taking the first steps in becoming leader-teachers themselves—learning from leaders who teach.

Improving the Leadership Skills of Those Who Teach

The third reason to implement a leaders-as-teachers approach is that it has valuable benefits not only for the learners but also for the leaders who teach. These benefits are gained in at least eight ways. First, leaders as teachers build strongly held beliefs that Noel Tichy calls leadership Teachable Points of View™.[1] In building these points of view, leader-teachers must hone and polish the way they articulate those ideas, strategies, and values about which they feel most strongly to be able teach and discuss them.

Second, leaders as teachers sharpen their leadership "saw." All effective leaders have points of view on topics vital to their success and the success of the organization they lead. For example, leadership points of view most frequently center on deeply held beliefs in areas such as

- keys to growing a business
- exceeding customer expectations
- how to achieve one's potential
- how teams or organizations do or can work at very high levels
- the values and ethics essential for success
- the role that teaching, coaching, or mentoring has in bringing out the best in others
- the role that courage and fierce resolve has had in achieving goals
- the place that humility has had in successes and effectiveness in working with others.

In BD's Advanced Leadership Development Program, the concept of leadership Teachable Points of View™ is utilized extensively. Program participants are asked to be prepared to identify and discuss a personal

---

1 Teachable Point of View is a registered trademark of Tichy Cohen Associates.

leadership Teachable Point of View™ they have on one or more of the topics listed above, or any other topic of importance to the participant that represents who they are as leaders—what they model, talk about, and therefore teach as part of their leadership role. As part of the teaching-learning process, the leaders who teach in the program also share their leadership Teachable Points of View™. Their process of preparing to do this and actually presenting their points of view frequently has the effect of what Steven Covey refers to as sharpening one's saw. It is an important honing and polishing process that has important developmental elements to it.

Third, leaders as teachers model desired behaviors. Many leader-teachers report that they are better able to model their desired leadership behaviors in their full-time role as a result of their preparation to teach and, then, actually teaching. When leaders prepare to teach, they learn the content of the program—either the actual specific content or the leadership, management, or functional/technical concepts that underlie the program—more deeply than they had previously known. These, of course, are for the most part the same concepts they are expected and expect of themselves to model in their actual work.

Fourth, leaders as teachers move out of their comfort zone. Job challenges of different types, sizes, shapes, and intensities are the "genetic material" that enable leaders to learn, grow, change, and develop. Teaching, for many leaders, is a very significant job challenge—it requires many leaders to step out of their comfort zone and to work across the grain of what they do best and most frequently. Sometimes leader-teachers have to teach or facilitate in content areas that are new, different, or even uncomfortable and strange for them. Experiences like this stimulate learning and development.

For experienced leader-teachers, teaching can also be a learning and developmental experience of a different kind. This occurs by building upon their existing strengths and by exposing them to people with whom they are not familiar. They frequently need to handle issues that arise in class with which they may not be comfortable and for which they may not have any time to prepare. Leader-teachers have to simultaneously be firm in their convictions as well as agile in their thinking and even spontaneous, depending on what presents itself in the classroom. Dealing with unpredictable questions, concerns, and issues helps teach important leadership lessons and skills. These types of teaching assignments that are out of their comfort zone are inherently developmental.

Fifth, leaders as teachers see new viewpoints. Leader-teachers often hear ideas and perspectives from other leader-teachers, and also students, that they would otherwise never have heard about but that provide a preview of something that is on the corporate horizon. By temporarily entering a different aspect of the organizational environment, in this case through the classroom, different relationships are formed and different viewpoints are experienced. Thus, it is healthy to periodically be able to view people and issues with a different lens and in different settings. Leader-teachers benefit tremendously by learning more about their own people and others whom they do not know but whom they are now teaching. Leader-teachers often report that they come away from their teaching assignments with a much more grounded approach to what is really going on in the organization and what others are thinking.

Sixth, leaders as teachers encourage self-improvement. Leaders regularly report that they feel a strong responsibility to model in their roles what they teach in a classroom. Whether it is a sense of responsibility, personal learning, pride, or even guilt, leader-teachers and the teams they lead benefit by tightening any gap between what they say and teach and what they do in their "real" roles. I have frequently heard individuals report that they are better leaders as a result of teaching. They are clearer about where they stand on issues, and they often improve their ability to speak on issues for which they take positions or feel strongly.

Consistently, leader-teachers report that they do not like the dissonance of saying and teaching one thing and doing something else. So almost all remove the dissonance by continuing to teach but by also improving how they perform day to day. As noted above, leader-teachers learn by coteaching with other leaders. They often share and discuss program content before, certainly during, and frequently after the program has been completed. Cotrainers provide each other with feedback. They make self-corrections to improve their own teaching. As trust builds, they make suggestions and exchange teaching feedback with fellow leader-teachers. Also, as noted above, a remarkable number of learning and developmental opportunities arise when leader-teachers take advantage of the available informal time to interact with fellow leader-teachers as well as students. Frequently, these opportunities occur during travel to and from programs, while leader-teachers are having discussions between themselves while students are involved in group or case study work, and during breaks and after-hour sessions.

Seventh, leaders as teachers expand social networks. It is particularly important that leader-teachers have built in opportunities to expand their internal informational and social networks by teaching others and by coteaching with other leaders.

Eighth, leaders as teachers are set up for future leadership roles. When leaders coteach with executives who have very considerable experience and responsibilities, they have natural opportunities to be more visible than they would otherwise, to interact with and also be viewed as valuable potential talent for the executive's organizations.

Strengthening Organizational Culture and Communications

The fourth reason to implement a leaders-as-teachers approach is that leader-teachers have the opportunity to strengthen their organization's culture and communications. This dynamic occurs in at least five ways. First, leader-teachers model desired organizational values. They can teach, talk about, model, and even write about desired organizational values, practices, aspirations, norms, and communications. The concept of setting the "leadership and ethical tone at the top" is vital in many respects. Leaders generally get the performance and behavior that they model and expect of others. By top, I do not mean just the CEO. There are many "tops" in organizations. For example, there are leaders of businesses; designated geographies such as divisions, territories, countries, and regions; and functional areas and teams. Associates and other managers and leaders are always scanning the organization to see what is acceptable and what is not. Leader-teachers have unique opportunities to explicitly and subtly serve as role models in their day-to-day responsibilities and when they teach.

Second, leader-teachers enhance the community of practice. They are part of important social networks within their organizations. These networks, which serve as cultural pathways and reinforcing mechanisms for organizational communications, have also come to be known as communities of practice with rich reservoirs of knowledge and professional experience for defined areas of expertise and responsibility. They also can serve as an ethical, moral, and values-based compass for acceptable and unacceptable behavior in the organization.

Company-wide, the leaders-as-teachers community of practice is an extraordinarily powerful force in organizational life. For instance, in the field of pharmacology, there is a concept known as drug potentiation. When one drug interacts with another drug, these is not always a $1 + 1 = 2$ effect. Instead, $1 + 1$ might equal the potentiated pharmacological effect of 3, 5, or more. In an analogous and very positive way, this is what happens when a strong social network and community of practice of leader-teachers is formed. Energy, sharing of information, and explicit and subtle messages are communicated throughout the organization by leader-teachers who help the business to achieve high levels of business performance while being supported by strong, values-based leadership.

Leader's Perspective

Bruce Stanley (BD's senior director for contracting operations) says: Being a leader-teacher has opened up new relationships and opportunities for me that normally would never have even surfaced. There is a certain level of camaraderie that exists among leader-teachers. We look out for each other and learn from each other in a nonthreatening environment. In most cases, this is where our peer coaches come from…. It has given me additional insights into the workings of the company. Being involved as a leader-teacher has given me access to experts around the world that I can call on for almost any business situation I find myself engrossed in. Likewise, I have become a resource in my field for other leader-teachers.

Third, leader-teachers encourage continuous learning. Through the actual process of serving as leader-teachers, leaders model the value of professional development and continuous learning. They also model that leaders are expected to teach, coach, and develop themselves and others on an ongoing basis. Leader-teachers send clear signals about the value of strengthening individual and organizational capability. Also, by encouraging others to become leader-teachers, those who already teach perpetuate and even expand this capability within their teams and throughout the enterprise.

There is an additional important benefit to consider. Leader-teachers are in an excellent position to provide the tools to raise issues and solve problems. For example, town meetings can be conducted during learning programs or as standalone sessions. They can model desired behavior while providing excellent opportunities to communicate important information. This can occur through both prepared statements and spontaneous responses to participant questions, assertions, concerns, and expressions of hope.

Fourth, leader-teachers drive organizational commitment. The very nature of certain program content describes, or is even the essence of, the actual desired business and organizational culture. When program participants experience modules—such as "good to great" principles, execution, decision making and problem solving, moral person/moral manager, and development of self and others—important messages are communicated. When leaders teach these sessions, these important messages and ideas can take on an even greater sense of urgency and commitment. These teaching settings also provide leader-teachers ideal moments to describe their teachable points. As noted above, examples of these leadership teachable points include setting and achieving high performance expectations; demonstrating the ethical tone at the top; the importance of developing oneself and others; ensuring high-quality processes and products; and the importance of strategic agility, teamwork, and collaboration.

Fifth, leader-teachers encourage cross-functional and cross-cultural ties. When leaders teach diverse groups of employees and other leaders, they have unique settings to stimulate cross-geographic, cross-business and cross-functional, and cross-identity group thinking and understanding. Left to their own natural dynamics, individuals, teams, and organizational units tend to be more closed than open in their communications and collaboration with other parts of the broader organization. By teaching heterogeneous groups or teaching in locations of the organization where they typically would not work or have much of a presence, leader-teachers often have a cross-fertilizing cultural effect when they lead and facilitate programs.

Promoting Positive Business and Organizational Change

The fifth reason to implement a leaders-as-teachers approach is that it enables leader-teachers to serve as catalysts for business and organizational change through their direct access to a wide range of learners. When leaders teach and coach, they are availing themselves of some of the most powerful levers for implementing change. At BD, leader-teachers are key supporters of change. The company adopted a common change model (John Kotter's eight-step model of change was added in 2000 as part of BDU's Leadership Development Program; BD's change initiative is discussed in depth in chapter 5). More than 2,000 managers and leaders have learned the model from some of BD's most senior, experienced, and credible executives. Kotter's (1996) principles are reinforced in training sessions with dozens of personalized BD examples presented or facilitated in case and group discussions. Kotter's change terms are used throughout the global organization. Change vocabulary—like "sense of urgency," "guiding coalition," and "generating short-term wins"—is commonplace at BD facilities around the world. By using specific examples and vocabulary related to change leadership and change initiatives, leader-teachers are employing both a direct and effective methodology to stimulate learning and affect a culture that is conducive to change.

Six Sigma

Change is also pushed through at BD with Six Sigma programs that serve as learning vehicles for important business or organizational change initiatives directly related to the company's performance and productivity. Hundreds of Six Sigma manufacturing and transactional projects have contributed in very important ways to the overall operational effectiveness of the company and are taught by certified BD leaders and professionals who use the design-measure-analyze-improve-control framework.

New Product Development

Almost all the training associated with BD's strategically linked change in the new product development process is led by company leader-teachers. In fact, the company's general managers are now accountable for the overall output of their businesses' product development efforts. This has required fundamentally rethinking, redesigning, and relearning a more effective product development process than previously existed. Business and functional leaders and professionals are driving this work at local levels and across the enterprise.

Other Ways Leaders Serve as Change Agents

As noted above, leaders who are subject matter experts can serve on program design or review teams for topics or programs that support business and organization change initiatives. Leader-teachers can also serve as guest speakers during programs or during organizational and team meetings; lead businesses, geographic organizations, enterprise processes, or function meetings; and integrate learning and change elements directly into their annual business plans. Finally, leader-teachers can use everyday opportunities to drive change initiatives and find teachable moments and convert them into learning experiences.

Reducing Costs by Leveraging Top Talent

The sixth and final reason to implement a leaders-as-teachers approach is that it drives numerous cost efficiencies by leveraging top talent. The leaders-as-teachers approach affords opportunities to deliver programs for "pennies on the dollar" compared with many other forms of delivery. In many cases, involving leader-teachers as subject matter experts eliminates or minimizes the need for expensive external consultants when internal capability is actually available for selected topics or courses.

In addition, a leaders-as-teachers process can be structured in ways that utilize the power of social networks, which, along with communities of practice, increase the likelihood of being able to easily import and export ideas, course materials, faculty, and the like across organizational boundaries. One of the many positive benefits of these practices is saving money through both organizational synergy and the reduction of duplication in the teaching-learning processes within organizations.

Even though a vibrant leaders-as-teachers process may be in place, utilization of external executive education programs still have an important educational role. The decision to send employees or leaders to external programs can be made more judiciously than if the internal leader-teacher capability were not in place.

◆ ◆ ◆

Implementation Activity: Checking the Value of Your Organization's Learning and Training Approach

The purpose of this activity is to compare the benefits of your organization's current approach to learning and training with the reasons and benefits for implementing a leaders-as-teachers approach.

Step 1: Think about your organization's approach to learning and training. List the primary reasons that your organization uses the approach that it does.

Step 2: What are the primary benefits derived from using your organization's current approach to learning and training?

Step 3: This chapter identified six primary reasons and benefits for implementing the leaders-as-teachers approach:

1. Helps drive business results
2. Stimulates the learning and development of leaders and associates
3. Improves the leadership skills of those who teach
4. Strengthens the organizational culture and communications
5. Promotes positive business and organizational change
6. Reduces cost by leveraging top talent.

When you compare these six reasons and benefits of your organization's current approach to learning and training with those of a leaders-as-teachers approach, what similarities and differences do you see? Make notes for each on a sheet of paper.

Step 4: Are there any benefits of a leaders-as-teachers approach that could be added to your organization's approach to learning and training? If so, what are they?

A Role for Every Leader

Dozens of Ways
Leaders Can Teach

See one, do one, teach one.
—Medical education mantra

◆ ◆ ◆

What's Inside This Chapter?

Now that you clearly understand the real benefits of implementing a
leaders-as-teachers program in your organization, this chapter offers some
concrete examples of the many ways leaders can participate in a leader-as-
teacher program. The placement of this chapter before the implementation chapters is designed to give you practical ideas to carry with you as you
read through the book. The point to remember is that a leaders-as-teachers
program can be as simple or complex as your organization can support.

The chapter includes more than 50 ways your leaders can teach, coach,
contribute to learning and training programs, and, more generally, contribute to organizational learning—organized into five broad categories
or approaches:

- Identifying learning needs and learning solution design
- Live teaching

- Teaching through the use of media and technology
- Preprogram and postprogram teaching and coaching to drive application and learning impact
- Recruiting, training, coaching, and mentoring leader-teachers.

At the end of the chapter, two activities can help you directly apply the major points in this section to your work setting by

- planning the implementation of your personal contributions as a leader-teacher
- determining how you can advance the overall leaders-as-teachers process in your organization.

◆ ◆ ◆

As discussed in chapter 2, there are at least six very practical reasons to implement a leaders-as-teachers program. Today's competitive work environment demands that organizations be disciplined and creative about how they facilitate the transfer of knowledge and experience. Winning organizations use learning, teaching, coaching, and mentoring in ways that their competition does not. They adopt innovative methods to learn, capture, and transfer important knowledge and skills. To stay ahead or get ahead, organizations must do this faster and with greater agility and staying power than their competition. Leaders who teach, coach, and mentor are at the epicenter of any business's ability to convert knowledge and skill gaps into unique assets and true competitive advantage. Leaders who are teachers and coaches enable this to happen through their individual teaching and their engagement and support for the leaders-as-teachers process with their teams and the broader organization.

There are dozens of ways to involve leaders as teachers. Leaders at any level can participate in leaders-as-teachers programs, and the following examples clearly demonstrate this principle. Review these suggestions and note which ones might work for you and for your organization and culture as you progress through the book.

Identifying Learning Needs and Learning Solution Design

This category includes leading or participating in the identification of the performance and learning issues, challenges, and opportunities that an organization faces. Having identified these needs and opportunities, this category also encompasses leaders' involvement in the design of the learning solutions and deliverables that will address them. Here are 15 examples to consider.

Actively participate in the identification of organizational performance and learning needs, challenges, and opportunities. Performance consultants and learning professionals usually lead this process. However, this task cannot and should not be done by performance consultants and learning professionals alone. These professionals provide valuable functional expertise, including the ability to create the process by which performance and learning needs and opportunities are assessed. Business and functional leaders have unique perspectives by virtue of their roles. They are also able to model the importance of ongoing performance improvement efforts and continuous learning. Their perspectives and active involvement add tremendous presence and importance to the identification of performance and learning needs and opportunities. In addition to being actively involved themselves, they can also assign members of their team and organization to work on this process and specific related tasks.

Use organizational surveys and sensing information as a catalyst for communicating and teaching about real work and real issues. This is a great source of needs and opportunities identification that leaders can charter, participate in, or receive once the data become available.

Participate in your company's business teams that plan the best ways to address performance and learning needs. Once performance needs, challenges, and opportunities are identified, there are many opportunities to collaborate with performance consultants, learning professionals, and other members of the business and functional organizations to determine how to best address the needs and opportunities. The product of such work and deliberations should be a specific plan that charts the path forward.

Serve on the company's corporate university team. Corporate university teams operate in a variety of ways and organizational structures. Their overall responsibility is to ensure that the learning needs of the organization are being met in highly effective ways across the enterprise. These teams frequently represent major business, functional, and geographic units and also include learning professionals. The team is typically led by the organization's chief learning officer or vice president of learning and development. Serving on this type of team is also an excellent development experience because of the challenges faced and the wide-angle view across the company that is required.

Serve as a program champion. A program champion is the individual who is selected or volunteers to lead the team that has responsibility for a designated program's design, choice of faculty trainers, staffing, oversight of the training of trainers, and continuous improvement. Program champions also support training coordinators, who administer the programs and schedule course offerings. Being a program champion or co-program champion is a large responsibility. It should only be taken on by someone who is passionate about the role and feels honored to be selected as the champion of a program that is important to your company.

There are several variations or forms of program champions. The ultimate role is program champion for the entire company. This individual has the overarching accountability for the program, as described above. There can also be local or regional program champions. These individuals drive the deployment and customization of the program at designated locations. There are those who oversee the program across an area as broad as a continent or country. These "local" champions serve on the program team that is led by the overall program champion.

Although program champions can be learning and development professionals, they are frequently business or functional leaders who are passionate about the program and the role that it serves in the company. Because it is a considerable responsibility, leaders might serve in the program champion role for a designated period, which, ideally, will be at least two years.

Such a role is also an excellent professional development experience because it spans the company, has unique challenges, and enables the champion to meet and interact with many people with whom he or she would not otherwise have the opportunity.

Serve as corporate university dean. Many corporate universities are organized into "colleges" that have the responsibility for common families or clusters of programs such as leadership, sales, business skills, manufacturing, compliance, and career development. Each of these colleges require an executive who works very closely with the corporate learning function to ensure that the portfolio of programs and resources in each curriculum-based college is aligned and integrated with the company's needs, is of high quality, and has sound plans for program implementation. Serving as a corporate university college dean is frequently part of an executive's set of broad business responsibilities. Sometimes, a

---

Leader's Perspective

Bruce Stanley (BD's senior director for contracting operations) explains his role as the global program champion for the company's Developing Your Career program in this way: In training teachers, I try to instill in them the same level of passion for coaching and listening that I have worked to develop in myself. I try to give them a foundation on which to build and develop their critical thinking skills.... I learned early to manage a global learning content team; it requires continuing outreach to folks who teach the material in all corners of the world. New ideas spring up everywhere. Many leader-teachers want to put their mark on the program. For the last four years, I have conducted annual detailed conference calls with all the trainers of Developing Your Career around the world. The purpose is to share what is new in the program, but, more important, to ask what each has done differently to make their sessions come alive. Often we discover that what begins as simple regional nuances have far-reaching applicability. We talk about the ideas as a group and then quickly implement them so as not to lose energy. I also work to keep the "juice" high. Programs can succeed or fail simply by the energy or lack thereof. I come to this unique role every day asking myself, what else can I do today to make the program stronger, more long lasting, and more life changing for all global associates. I never stop asking myself these questions. We will try almost anything if it has merit.

---

very senior learning and development or talent management leader will head one of the colleges within the corporate university.

Lead or co-lead the development of a new program. Leaders might be motivated for several reasons to serve in this role. The leader could simply be deeply interested in the program and its content. He or she could have previously taught a similar program in your or another organization. The program could advance a specific business agenda for which the leader has responsibility. Regardless of the motivation, leaders add tremendously valuable experience, insights, and points of view in the new program development process. This type of involvement almost always occurs in conjunction with learning professionals and sometimes with external vendors. These valuable partnerships add to the leadership and professional development efforts of an organization and advance areas such as leadership, management, business skills, business acumen, specific functional skills and knowledge, sales, and personal career development.

Involve leaders in customized program design. In designing these tailored programs, it is important to involve a variety of perspectives, especially those of the end users, because these programs are created or an existing program is modified to address the carefully identified needs of a specific population. This type of leader involvement adds to the quality of programs, builds business commitment, and establishes content knowledge for others who might later teach the program.

Serve as subject matter experts working in a live or virtual fashion to either help design or teach a program. A team approach to program development is very important for a variety of reasons. Having one or two subject matter experts involved in this process is essential. Their years of experience and the respect they have built in the organization add the credibility that is vital to the content of programs. One subject matter expert personally wrote several case studies that were used in a senior-level leadership program. These experts may contribute through in-person working groups that meet at scheduled times or through a variety of virtual mechanisms that span geographies and time zones. Today's technologies allow for a flexibility in program design that never existed in previous years. The asynchronous editing of documents, web-based video presentations, and a continuous expansion of topic-specific wikis are only three ways that subject matter experts can contribute to program development and the creation of performance support tools.

Advise on the selection of vendors, and then teach in-licensed programs. Some programs are developed by teams consisting of members who are part of the company. Other programs are purchased and licensed from external vendors. The selection of the right vendors and the programs that will have the best business and cultural fit can make all the difference for eventual acceptance and success. Business and functional leaders' input and perspective on the appropriateness, quality, and ways to customize the program through collaboration with the vendor adds greatly to organizational acceptance. The involvement of key leaders and professionals in vendor and program selection also makes it much more likely that they will be engaged teachers and facilitators.

Serve as sounding boards and feedback providers for continuous improvement efforts of programs. Respected leaders with a range of business, geographic, and functional experience add valuable points of view that keep programs updated and relevant. Involvement in this type of activity usually requires only short periods of time. Leaders might read and respond to written program materials. They might actually experience the program as a participant or as a teacher and then add their perspective. They could also be interviewed by a program champion or learning professional to quickly gain insights from the leader about the program's content or instructional process.

Participate in new program development "shakedowns." Shakedowns are half- to full-day comprehensive reviews of content and instructional methods usually conducted about six weeks before launching a new program. Leaders' and professionals' points of view at this critical point in the program's development help to ensure a successful launch of a highly effective and valuable program. I do not support the notion of "pilot programs." Too frequently, they serve as an excuse for an inadequately developed or strategically misaligned program. The shakedown helps to identify strengths and areas for improvement that might only be identified in a pilot at a point when a program begins to develop its own reputation. The role of experienced leader-teachers in the shakedown process is essential. There is no substitute for their perspective, perceptive questions, and sage counsel.

Swap and share your organization's best learning ideas. Many organizations develop nearsighted, silo-like behaviors, which impede the horizontal flow of information and resources across organizational boundaries. When leaders and professionals who represent different organizational units work together on learning initiatives, program development, and coteaching, these business-limiting behaviors are reduced or disappear. They share information and, in so doing, strengthen the organization. These are just some of the ways that leaders serving as teachers have a natural silo-busting effect in the organization.

Facilitate "strategic or organizational profiles." This is a process by which well-trained and highly respected leaders facilitate a structured process that results in the identification of strategies and plans essential to a specific part of the company or the company as a whole.

Participate in a strategic or organizational profiling session and share what you know. Rather than lead or facilitate the development of strategic and organizational profiles, leaders can participate in the profiling session and provide their input on an identified topic or challenge that is the session's focus.

Live Teaching

This category includes a wide array of ways that leaders can contribute as teachers and facilitators of learning in face-to-face learning sessions. Here are 17 examples to consider.

Leader's Perspective

Krista Thompson (BD's vice president and general manager, global health) describes a unique contribution that she and her team made in their efforts in an underdeveloped part of the world: Truly being a global leader means constantly learning and teaching. It is a positive feedback cycle. There is a global leadership gap, and leaders serving as teachers is a great way to start to address this problem. As an example, I had the opportunity to use the leaders-as-teachers approach with the Ministry of Health leaders in Ghana. It was a powerful experience in transforming knowledge that will be used in a whole new environment.

Individually teaching sections or modules of the program. This is the classic way that leaders contribute as teachers. Whether it is a short, 30-minute section of a course or teaching major parts of a multiday leadership program, this is the essence of leaders sharing their experience and points of view with other professionals and leaders in their organization.

Coteaching the major parts of a program. I recommend that leaders coteach programs rather than teaching alone. Coteaching allows for cross-fertilization of ideas with students and faculty, knowledge sharing, and feedback between the leader-teachers. It also adds additional perspectives and a change in style and pace for the participants. Most important, coteaching provides contingency planning if any business or personal emergencies interfere with the ability of a leader to teach.

Speaking and teaching about personal leadership Teachable Points of View™. As mentioned in chapter 2, leadership Teachable Points of View™ represent some of the most important professional values and deeply held beliefs about topics that are vital to that leader and the business. These perspectives potentially have great relevance to the students.

Leader's Perspective

John Hanson (executive vice president international, BD) says: I'm often asked why I dedicate three weeks a year to BD University, particularly the Leadership Development Program and Advanced Leadership Development Program. Europe is a growing and exciting region. We have more than 5,000 associates engaged in helping us become a "Great Company," stretching from the Nordic countries down to Africa and from the United Kingdom across to the Middle East. Developing and growing talent, let alone communicating and implementing our strategy, in such a diverse and multicultural region can be a formidable challenge. I find the opportunity to bring associates together from different countries, disciplines, and at different developmental stages of their career in a focused Leadership Development Program to be a very effective catalyst. The individual interaction around learning and development is a very powerful and motivational mechanism to grow our key people. It's also a two-way learning process for me, and provides a unique opportunity to sense the future potential for leadership roles.

Serving as a lunchtime guest speaker on the theme of the program or by teaching "the company orthodoxy" (strategy, goals and objectives, company values). In usually a 30- to 60-minute period of time, leaders have a wonderful opportunity to share their perspectives and experiences on the topic of the program— for example, personal career management, business execution, business ethics. In other types of programs, the leader might communicate information about the company's growth strategies or explain the organization's key priorities and challenges.

Speaking at "town meetings" during programs or at separately scheduled town meeting sessions. Town meetings provide a natural forum for information exchange and for teaching and learning to occur. The typical length of these sessions is about 45 to 90 minutes. These are superb opportunities for senior leaders and executives to connect with a class or a larger group of associates. Ed Ludwig, BD's chairman and CEO, is a master of town meetings. Often in person and occasionally by videoconferencing or teleconferencing from halfway around the world, I have seen Ed conduct powerful town meetings during offsite residential leadership development programs on dozens of occasions. Ed also holds regularly scheduled quarterly, company-wide town meetings that coincide with financial reporting periods. These are usually held live with several hundred associates at the corporate headquarters, while other managers and associates are able to call in with the aid of operator-assisted lines from around the globe. A common format for town meetings consists of opening comments by the leader-teacher followed by unrehearsed questions and answers.

Facilitating town meetings. For town meetings to be successful, some preparation of both the speaker and of the class is important. This consists of choosing, inviting, and preparing the leader who is the focus of the meeting. I often will ask the CEO or, alternatively, other senior executives to speak. Town meetings can be highly successful with one executive or with as many as two or three speaking. I do not like to go beyond three executives because it is important for each to have adequate "airtime" with the class.

It is also important to prepare the class for the town meeting. This usually consists of establishing several guidelines about the conduct of the session. I ask all class members to come to the meeting with at least one question that they have thought about and would be willing to ask. I always ask one person to volunteer to ask the first question to avoid that predictable awkward period when everyone is wondering who will raise his or her hand first with a question. It only takes an initial question to be asked and the remainder of the meeting usually flows smoothly. Occasionally, the facilitator of the meeting may ask a clarifying question that will help to better link the speaker's comments to an issue that has come up. If the meeting is being held as part of a multiday session, I will often brief the executive beforehand about any key topics or issues that have been discussed or are on a "parking lot" list waiting to be addressed.

Coaching participants during the program. This could occur during small group work and, under the certain conditions, with the larger class watching and listening as part of an exercise or at just the right teach-able moment.

Facilitating peer coaching, peer assists, and peer teaching. Each of these methods taps into the experience and creative problem-solving capability of fellow learners in a class. These methods empower each learner in a class to as-sume a coaching, teaching, or facilitating role for short periods of time. Peer coaching is usually done in groups of threes. Each person has equal time during three successive rounds to be the focus of two peers to help think through an identified issue, topic, or challenge. Peer assists are a variation on peer coaching; one person's challenge becomes the focus of the entire class and benefits from the wave of ideas that is generated. Peer teaching can take a number of forms. It essentially consists of one person or, more commonly, small groups within a class, teaching each other what they know about an identified topic.

Offline teaching and coaching during programs. These are informal teaching mo-ments during breaks, meals, and social time. More than at any other time, I witnessed and learned the power of this offline teaching and coach-ing approach from John Hanson, who is the executive vice president, international, at BD. John uses almost every moment to teach and coach during leadership development programs. He often has created lists of people who he wants to spend time with and topics that he wishes or needs to discuss, even before the class sessions begins. Those lists often grow as the class progresses. It is common for John to meet with small groups or individually with class participants before and after sessions, during breaks and meals, and during what I call "walks and talks" in off hours when class is not in session. This is an example of full involvement in the teaching, coaching, and learning process by a senior executive. Everybody benefits and feels valued because of the separate time they are able to get with an important leader. This offline coaching is quite powerful. It also serves as valuable role-modeling behavior for others.

Teaching by "schmoozing" during a program (getting a message across by informally interacting and building relationships). This is a variation on offline teaching and coaching. Leaders can positively influence the learning and thinking process of program participants through usually unplanned informal interactions throughout the program. These are often brief, several-minute interactions that take advantage of the access to class participants during informal periods before, during, and after class. It brings out the humanity in leaders. Whether it is working out together, sharing a meal, or laughing at a joke, these are all opportunities to get points across and build relationships with others in the organization.

Being interviewed by another leader-teacher, facilitator, or group on a topic. This is an easy and powerful way to teach, model, and communicate important information and personal leadership Teachable Points of View™. The unrehearsed, spontaneous nature of the interview frequently conveys candor and credibility as important topics are discussed.

Tackling tough "parking lot" issues in class. A common teaching and facilitation method is to keep a running list of follow-up topics that need to be addressed before a program ends. These issues often arise at times during the program when it would be awkward or distracting to discuss them at that particular point in the program. Thus the ideas get "parked," usually by posting it on a flip chart and keeping it very visible until it is addressed later in the program. Sometimes, the assigned leader-teachers for the class tackle the topics. It is also common that certain issues may be very sensitive and might require the expertise of a company resource, such as a human resources leader or possibly a senior executive who can address the issue or question. Depending on the type of program, it is sometimes advisable to have one of these individuals on call for an hour during the program to ensure that the parking lot topics are voiced and that participants in the program have responsible answers to questions and concerns they have raised.

Real-time commentary or coaching of implementation or action plans as they are described in small or large group settings. In many programs, participants are asked to develop action or implementation plans. Program participants can be organized as peers to coach these plans, thus serving as leader-teachers as well as learners. And those leaders who are teaching the program can also provide real-time coaching and commentary as a half-dozen or so plans are described to the class participants by those who have developed them.

Facilitating new leader and team "onboarding" or assimilation processes and sessions. Increasingly, many organizations have implemented formal leadership onboarding processes to help newly appointed or promoted managers and leaders achieve a smooth landing in their roles and with their teams. One of these approaches is the new leader and team assimilation process, which is facilitated by a trained third party. With the proper training, leader-teachers can facilitate these important sessions. Performing this facilitative role helps the new leader and his or her team. The facilitator also benefits by gaining insights into the leadership transition process that can be helpful the next time he or she is in that situation.

Facilitating and coaching longer-term action learning projects. These projects are typically linked to important current or projected challenges and opportunities that the company faces. Participants usually work in small teams to diagnose the problem and then recommend a course of action to the organization's senior leadership.

Facilitating and teaching by using reaction sheets. Reaction sheets can be used in many settings. I especially like them in conjunction with prework reading assignments. They can also be used as an in-class activity. These sheets usually consist of three to six questions that help to deepen the learner's understanding of the prereading assignment. A reaction sheet can also consist of an exercise that needs to be completed or an opportunity to write about a small case, a challenge, or a dilemma that needs resolution. Reaction sheets make teaching and facilitation easier than it might otherwise be. They prime the pump for effective teaching and learning.

Facilitating and teaching by using reaction questions. Well-designed reaction questions enrich the learning process. Prepare several questions that you can use to begin the discussion of a prework or in-class reaction sheet. These questions help to deepen understanding and can also be used as a catalyst to stimulate creative thinking and problem solving. Leader-teachers love the potent combination of reaction sheets and follow-up reaction questions—it's relatively easy to use for those who know a topic and want to stimulate an active teaching and learning process.

Using Media and Technology to Teach

In today's technology-rich world, there are many ways that business, functional, and leadership learning is accessible to learners with a mere point and click. The growth of a wide variety of enabling technologies has greatly expanded the possible ways that experts' and leaders' knowledge, experience, and coaching can be made available to learners on an immediate, need-to-know basis. Here are 11 examples to consider.

Using technology such as intranet and Internet sites, blogs, streaming videos, and wikis. These represent a broad range of information sharing for social networks and communities of practice as well as methods that support broader individual learning and performance needs. The access to material and information that is now available for just-in-time learning and for immediate performance support would have been almost unimaginable 15 or 20 years ago. Leader-teachers have numerous opportunities to contribute to the information that is made available through these and other technology vehicles. For example, they can write down information. Or leader-teachers can designate certain information and program content to be read, watched, or experienced. Or they can create communities of practice, which are digitally linked for knowledge and resource sharing.

Teleconferencing. The practice of using teleconferences for learning and performance support has been available for years. Teleconferencing remains one of the simplest, most reliable technologies for knowledge transfer. This technology can be used for one-to-one and group teaching, coaching, and information sharing. With the enormous advances in mobile telephone technology and use, other possibilities seem almost endless.

Videoconferencing. Videoconferencing is a step up in technology, visual access, and personalization from teleconferencing. Yet, like teleconferencing, videoconferencing can be used for one-to-one and group teaching, coaching, and information sharing. Satellite and fiber-optic capabilities have made this technology essentially instantaneous from one's computer-enabled work station, from dedicated videoconferencing rooms, from home, or as one travels. Videoconferencing is very time- and cost-effective when compared with travel.

Providing input for use in e-enabled, or technology-enabled, learning programs and platforms. A key role for leader-teachers in the technology arena is to be sources of content and subject matter expertise. Learning technologists are able to convert this input into e-enabled programs and resources that are then made available when needed to individual learners (asynchronous) or to be used at the same time with others (synchronous).

Participating in blended learning solutions. Blended learning solutions involve the integration of technology-enabled learning with some form of live teaching and learning. There are many variations of blended solutions. For example, a leadership program might include a 20-minute streaming video or DVD clip with the CEO speaking on company performance and its strategic goals for the upcoming year. The CEO may not be able to be at the session, but another senior leader in the organization may then lead a strategy learning session that uses the 20-minute segment as the catalyst for that module of the program.

Teaching through Webinars. A common teaching and learning technology that has developed over the past decade is the use of Webinars. Enabled by the power of the Internet, leader-teachers are now able to reach learners across a company, across countries, and across time zones through the use of Webinars. Webinars are extremely cost-effective and relatively easy to prepare. With some exceptions, they should generally be limited to approximately 60 to 90 minutes. Webinars can be experienced live or can be archived and accessed at a more convenient or relevant time. Webinars allow for some back-and-forth interaction.

Podcasts. Podcasts have some of the same characteristics as Webinars. A difference is the even greater convenience of being able to download the content to an iPod or MP3 device. Several common ways that leader-teachers can provide input to podcasts are to deliver a lecture or key messages or to be interviewed either alone or as part of a panel. I recently experienced one of the newest advancements in the use of podcasts. This involves conference speakers calling into a service and recording a five- to 10-minute message that outlines the key points of their sessions. Minutes later, the messages appear on a program wiki that conference attendees can very easily access. This technology has many potential applications for asynchronous, self-paced learning.

Facilitating and teaching business and functional simulations and games. Simulations have existed for many years. Not all digital games are simulations. Over the past 20 years, the use of computer-enabled games and business simulations has grown significantly. These learning platforms can be used as digital metaphors and catalysts for learning or comprehensive simulations for a wide range of roles and business situations. For example, a number of simulations have been developed where learners can assume the role of a general manager who has the responsibility to run an entire business. There are also many types of customized and noncustomized simulations that are functionally specific. Examples include those in the fields of manufacturing, project management, supply chain management, operational business processes, pharmaceutical drug development, engineering, and sales. Leader-teachers can be trained to facilitate and teach using the simulation experience as the primary learning platform. And their input during the design and testing phase of the simulation is very valuable.

Simulators. In today's world of commercially available virtual reality games, many children and adults have considerable experience with packages that test skills, thinking, mental agility, and eye-hand coordination. From a digital evolutionary perspective, the precursor to these relatively inexpensive devices and games, which are intended primarily for entertainment and fun, were the sophisticated simulators that have been used in training for high-skill and precision occupations for years.

Ironically, today's simulators have, in turn, also benefited from the tremendous advances in technology-based games. Contemporary simulators are highly sophisticated, technical units where real-work scenarios are practiced and tested in the world of virtual reality. This type of technology enables many challenging variables to be encountered and dealt with in an instant. Pilots, astronauts, project managers, engineers, submariners, large machine and equipment operators, and surgeons are examples of occupations where simulators have been used for years. There are important roles for leader-teachers even when this level of technology is used.

The development of simulators requires subject matter experts to provide input and ultimately to approve and periodically revise the content of the technology. Simulators can be used in a variety of blended learning solutions. For example, it is important to have student's simulator performance assessed and debriefed by experts to help the student crystallize the learning experience and improve performance.

Teaching/facilitating in virtual meetings. This is most often done through either teleconferences or videoconferences.

Second Life. A much newer form of simulations and virtual reality is the medium known as Second Life. This is a very sophisticated virtual world that is increasingly being used for learning and performance improvement purposes. Leader-teachers' expertise can be used as the basis of learning scenarios in Second Life, as well as serve as learning facilitators using Second Life as the supporting medium. Leader-teachers can also debrief learning during phases or sessions within Second Life.

Preprogram and Postprogram Teaching and Coaching to Drive Application and Learning Impact

A number of factors influence the effectiveness and the ultimate impact of learning on individual and business performance. Certainly, the timing and effectiveness of the live teaching or technology-enabled learning experience are both essential factors as is the quality of the content. And both preprogram and postprogram coaching, as well as support and accountability provided by the learner's manager, is a key determinant in learning retention and the all-important conversion of learning into action. Here are five examples to consider.

Leaders coaching participants before the program to set expectations for learning and to raise the accountability for the postprogram implementation of action plans. Too frequently, participants are simply asked to show up or are assigned to participate in a training session without any idea why they are there. When this happens, significant learning opportunities have already been lost. Preprogram coaching makes a very large difference in setting the expectations for both learning and, more important, the accountability for the implementation of the learning content following the learning event.

> **Leader's Perspective**
> Susan Luthy (vice president, corporate/human resources, BD) says: As a leader-teacher, I often learn more than my students. First, when preparing for the classroom, I study the material closely. Second, I have learned to facilitate in a manner that brings out the best from the people in the class. While in class, I learn about corners of the organization where I don't ordinarily work. Most important, in teaching situations, I learn what works for others and what doesn't. They share life experiences and tell stories that have great impact. They inform me of the things that really made a positive difference in their lives. As a leader in a new role, I have heard from people all around the world what works for them and what doesn't when they are working with a new leader. I know these insights continuously guide me to be a more effective and better leader.

Leaders coaching participants after the program to ensure the likelihood of sustained learning and the effective implementation of action plans. Just as too many participants can attend training programs or participate in an e-enabled event without understanding why, all too frequently there is little, if any, postevent coaching and expectation setting by the participant's report-to leader. When coaching and accountability for the implementation of learning is provided, the likelihood increases of learning retention and the successful implementation of professional development and action plans. Preevent and postevent learning event coaching is a leader-teacher role that can be an institutionalized expectation. Both preprogram and postprogram coaching consistently makes a big difference in the effectiveness of learning processes.

Personalize key messages learned during a program and teach others following the program. There are many opportunities to reinforce and embed key messages with your team following programs you have attended. For example, you can create or take advantage of naturally occurring "teachable moments" by modeling and discussing an important idea or a personal leadership Teachable Point of View™ at just the right time. This can introduce an idea to others or provide a booster shot to reinforce earlier or ongoing learning. Another way is to include the idea or concept from the program as part of a performance, professional development, or team objective for you and possibly your team.

Talk about an important concept at your team meetings or in broader organizational or town meetings. You can follow up with each of your direct reports after your learning experience and share the importance that a particular concept has had on you. You could also discuss the points you wish to reinforce with your peers, colleagues, and even your boss. Technology can help you as well by making your ideas available to those to whom you wish to target your message.

Writing is another way to reinforce important ideas. This could be as simple as scribing reinforcing notes to one or more individuals who you feel could benefit from the idea or from your coaching. You could also write in internal communication vehicles like newsletters, in performance aids, and in new or updated training materials.

Recruiting, Training, Coaching, and Mentoring Leader-Teachers

This category focuses on the role of experienced leader-teachers and learning professionals to recruit, train, coach, and mentor new and less-experienced leader-teachers. Here are four examples to consider.

The recruitment, selection, and preparation of leader-teachers. This topic will be discussed in detail in chapter 6. Suffice it to say at this point that today's leader-teachers have the most important role to play to ensure that there are generations of leader-teachers that will follow them. Their personal motivation, engagement, and valuing of teaching and coaching set a very powerful business and cultural tone for the organization. These factors, combined with their content expertise and teaching experience, are the foundation upon which to recruit, select, and teach others who aspire to have their level of expertise as well as the very real respect they have earned from others.

In-program coaching of other leader-teachers. This can occur very naturally when coteaching or team teaching by working closely, in a supportive and developmental manner, with colleagues who may have less teaching experience or who wish to build their confidence as leader-teachers.

Mentoring leader-teachers. This mentoring of leader-teachers can occur in several forms. It can take place over a specified period of time expressly to help one person or a small cohort become effective in their role as leader-teachers. It can also occur by working with one or more leader-teachers on their broader developmental and career growth.

Ongoing coaching of associates and other leaders. Coaching is not limited to coaching other leader-teachers. Actually, a prime example of leaders serving as teachers on a daily basis is to approach their leadership role as a coaching role—coaching your team for strong performance and for ongoing professional development.

◆ ◆ ◆

Implementation Activity 1: How Can I Contribute as a Leader-Teacher?

This activity is a personal opportunity search designed to help you determine at least two ways that you can contribute as a leader-teacher or to expand the ways in which you already contribute. It will also enable you to develop a plan to take action on the opportunities you identify to be a leader-teacher or to expand the ways you may already be contributing as a leader-teacher.

This chapter has described five categories and more than 50 ways in which leaders can serve as teachers and coaches. Follow these steps:

1. Review the five categories and the several dozen methods that are described in this chapter.
2. List three to six methods that are possible ways for you to contribute or to expand the ways you may already contribute as a leader-teacher.
3. Of the three to six possible methods, which two appeal to you the most or do you think would be the best fit for you, given your skills, interests, and experience?
4. For each of the two methods or approaches that you selected in step 3, in what program(s) or settings(s) would you like to use these methods, and by when?
5. What steps or progressions would help you to best prepare to teach using each of these methods?
6. What is the first step you will take to include these methods as part of your leader-teacher set of capabilities, and by when?

Implementation Activity 2: How Can I Advance the Leaders-as-Teachers Process?

This activity is an organizational opportunity search designed to help you determine one or two ways in which you can help advance the overall approach to making the leaders-as-teachers process an integral part of your organization's business, learning, and development strategies. It will enable you to develop a plan for acting on the opportunities you identified to help make this process an integral part of your organization's strategies.

Leaders can individually contribute as teachers and coaches in many very important ways. Answer these questions:

1. In addition to your individual efforts to teach and coach, what are one or two actions that you are willing to take that will help advance the overall support and engagement of the leaders-as-teachers process with teams or parts of the organization that you lead or of which you are a part?
2. Who else will you involve, and by when?
3. How will your team or organization benefit from your efforts?
4. What are the first steps you will take, and by what date?

Chapter 4

Yes, Where You Work!

Why Leaders Want to Teach and Come Back for More

Winning organizations are teaching organizations.
—Noel Tichy

Think of deeply embedded life interest as a geothermal pool of superheated water. It will rise to the surface in one place as a hot spring and in another as a geyser. But beneath the surface—at the core of the individual—the pool is constantly bubbling. Deeply embedded life interests always seem to find expression, even if a person has to change jobs—or careers— for that to happen.
—Tim Butler and Jim Waldroop

♦ ♦ ♦

What's Inside This Chapter?

Chapter 3 demonstrated the many ways in which leaders can serve as teachers. Now it is time to start building your own version of a leaders-as-teachers program. The premise of this chapter is that the motivation to teach exists in many organizational leaders but that tapping into that energy requires some knowledge and finesse. This chapter offers guidance on attracting and engaging leaders to serve as teachers by appealing to aspects of human nature that support the desire to participate in a leaders-as-teachers program. BD found its insights into this critical aspect of building a leaders-as-teachers program in the work of leadership, career, and organizational development experts Noel Tichy, Bernard Haldane, and Tim Butler and Jim Waldroop.

◆ ◆ ◆

The Influence of Noel Tichy's Work

Noel Tichy pioneered the leaders-as-teachers concept and has written directly about the power of leaders serving as teachers. He is a professor of organizational behavior and human resource management at the University of Michigan. He directs the Global Leadership Partnership, and he is a worldwide adviser to CEOs on leadership and transformation. He worked for Jack Welch in establishing GE's famed leadership development programs and processes at the Crotonville Center.

Tichy's pioneering writing on the importance and nature of teaching organizations has been published in a number of texts and articles. In *The Leadership Engine* (1997), *The Cycle of Leadership* (2002), and "The Teaching Organization" (1998), he provides the conceptual framework to support a leaders-as-teachers approach. He presents a fundamental premise of leaders as teachers in *The Leadership Engine:*

> Winning Organizations are teaching organizations.... The winning organizations and people who do this well come in all shapes, sizes and nationalities, and can be found in any industry. The goods and services they produce and the strategies and tactics they employ are widely divergent. But they all share a set of four fundamentals. First, leaders with a proven track record of success take direct responsibility for the development of other leaders.
>
> Second, leaders who develop other leaders have teachable points of view in the specific areas of ideas, values and something that I call E-cubed—emotional energy and edge. Winning leaders/teachers have ideas that they can articulate and teach

to others about both how to make the organization successful in the marketplace and how to develop other leaders. They have teachable values about the kinds of behavior that will lead to organizational and personal success. They deliberately generate positive emotional energy in others. And they demonstrate and encourage others to demonstrate edge, which is the ability to face reality and make tough decisions.

Third, leaders embody their teachable points of view in living stories. They tell stories about their pasts that explain their learning experiences and their beliefs. And they create stories about the future of their organizations that encourage others, both emotionally and intellectually, to attain the winning future that they describe.

Fourth and finally, because winning leaders invest considerable time developing other leaders, they have well-defined methodologies and coaching and teaching techniques. Among

---

Leader's Perspective

Jay Glasscock (country general manager, BD) says: Being a leader-teacher at BD has been an extremely rewarding experience for me. First and most important, I get a huge amount of leadership energy from teaching. The dynamic between teacher and student in the classroom is quite different from the dynamic of the typical meeting room as it provides for a unique opportunity to debate and further refine our strategy in an open, collaborative manner. Preparing for a class drives me to get clear on my leadership point of view, and teaching in a classroom allows me to personalize my message and further explain why the company is on a particular path. Teaching also provides a rare opportunity to interact with future leaders in the organization and witness firsthand their intellectual horsepower, their ability to build on others' ideas, and their learning agility. Teaching has definitely taught me to listen more closely as a leader; there are many insights and great ideas that come from both the classroom and back in the office. I have learned to keep a very open mind on where we are leading the organization and relearned the power of involving our associates at every level as we build a great organization.

these is the willingness to admit mistakes and show their vulnerabilities in order to serve as effective role models for others. (Tichy 1997, 3–4)

In *The Cycle of Leadership*, Tichy describes four critical success factors for teaching organizations:

- *Reliance on alignment through dialogue, not authority....* Teaching organizations challenge traditional ideas of authority.... Teaching organizations expect great insights to come from all levels of the organization.
- *Commitment and contribution by all employees....* Since everyone is heard and more important, expected to teach others, they have direct input into the organization's overall direction.
- *Level of knowledge creation....* The competitive edge of teaching organizations is that they generate more knowledge and intellectual capital.
- *Sharing best practices and knowledge across all boundaries....* People who create fiefdoms or insulate themselves from new ideas are the bane of teaching organizations.... Good ideas can come from anywhere. By definition, this means that leaders are simultaneously learning while simultaneously teaching others. (Tichy 2002, 294)

Tichy also describes the characteristics of world-class leader-teachers in *The Cycle of Leadership:*

- Is a good listener
- Is passionate about the subject
- Knows the subject well
- Tells stories and uses practical examples
- Provides context for why the subject is relevant to the learner
- Makes a personal connection to the topic
- Takes time to understand learner's capabilities
- Is open to learning from the student
- Makes teaching and learning interactive—what Tichy calls the virtuous teaching cycle

- Can use visual, audible, and physical teaching tools effectively
- Sincerely cares about whether the learner understands
- Never gives up, gets frustrated or bored (Tichy 2002, 296).

Takeaways from Tichy's Work

Clearly, Tichy's work provides many of the fundamental concepts for building any leaders-as-teachers program. In building BD's leaders-as-teachers approach, we took maximum advantage of his writings. Let's look at the 11 principal takeaways from Tichy's work that BD used to build its leaders-as-teachers program.

Set the bar high for the leaders-as-teachers program. Winning organizations are teaching as well as learning organizations. Continuous learning and improvement must be one of the highest and most rewarded priorities for current and future business growth.

Ensure CEO total commitment to the leaders-as-teachers program. The tone at the top is set most powerfully when the CEO and the senior management team model by positive action their own role in implementing the leaders-as-teachers approach. CEOs, executive vice presidents, and senior vice presidents send the right message when they take time from their busy schedules to teach in an auditorium or classroom, or they make informal teaching and coaching part of their daily leadership style. The positive role model offered by these leaders gives other leaders in the organization permission to emulate their behavior.

Make the leaders-as-teachers program an expected part of the leader's job. Leaders and their organizations must consider teaching an expected part of any leader's role and set aside time to teach, coach, and mentor. In addition to embracing the idea of teaching and learning as an organizational value, truly committed organizations directly link this support to their core human resource practices. This support link is most commonly expressed by embedding in their organization's performance management process (and yes, even their compensation and talent management practices) an expectation to participate in a leaders-as-teachers program. At BD, the individual's role as a leader-teacher is sometimes noted in organizational announcements when a leader is promoted. What better way to promote the organization's commitment to leaders as teachers!

Another way to demonstrate organizational support is to include active participation in the leaders-as-teachers approach as a criterion in the succession planning and talent review processes. In organizations where being a leader-teacher is truly important, leaders send a clear message that they believe there is a positive relationship between teaching, learning, organizational engagement, and team and organizational performance.

Leader-teachers need to take an active role in the development of others. Leaders must take an active role in the development of other leaders and associates. Career experts agree that the first level of responsibility for ongoing learning and personal career development begins with the individual. Yet a committed leader-teacher and coach with a real interest in the growth and development of others is an important part of an individual's journey toward success, whether that help is informal or formal teaching, coaching, or advising and mentoring.

Develop a Teachable Point of View™ for the leaders-as-teachers program. Leaders must develop their own personal Teachable Points of View™ and expect the same from other developing leaders. These points of view can be based on a wide range of issues, including individual and team effectiveness, business success, and values and ethically based conduct. However, leaders must understand the importance of consistency between their words and actions, because not living up to your words is viewed as inconsistent or even hypocritical.

Develop vivid stores to communicate a Teachable Point of View™ in the leaders-as-teachers program. Leadership Teachable Points of View™ come to life in

---

Leader's Perspective

Joe Toto (director of leadership development and learning, BD) says: There is no question that leaders who teach at BD find that the experience has improved their own leadership capabilities. They report that it raises the bar for the need to model the principles and concepts they teach, and they are often motivated to study deeper on their own in the subjects they teach.

---

the form of stories, anecdotes, and career reflections that have a personal and authentic feel. Leader-teachers use these stories in day-to-day interactions with leaders who have strongly held points of view as well as in classroom situations. These stories make a Teachable Point of View™ a memorable and powerful learning tool.

For example, some years ago I was involved in a business meeting that had bogged down due to the topic's complex nature and the ultimate financial commitment of the organization. After almost three hours of hand-wringing discussions, the president of the organization joined us and, after listening to our recap of our discussion, simply said, "Do the right thing, always do the right thing." This simple phrase helped us take action and feel confident about our decision that day. Twenty years later, this is just one of many leadership Teachable Points of View™ stories I tell in my leadership programs and is a good example of how one executive's sage counsel can continue to influence others for years to come.

Proactively develop teaching, coaching, and mentoring skills for the leaders-as-teachers program. Only a small percentage of managers and leaders have innate teaching, coaching, and mentoring skills. Like most management and leadership skills, only practice and proactive development can broaden these skills. And leaders who take the time to develop these skills in themselves should expect the same from others who have responsibility for people and teams. It takes committed action on the part of many to sustain a teaching-learning cycle, but this is how learning and teaching organizations evolve.

Constructively challenge the status quo with the leaders-as-teachers program. Regular teaching, coaching, and learning is one way to avoid an organization's natural tendency to get comfortable in set ways of behaving and thinking. Thriving organizations counter this natural tendency to become complacent with active leaders-as-teachers programs that tend to challenge the status quo. Effective leader-teachers can spark innovative thinking and creative problem solving through skillful teaching and facilitation and through their unique contact with other leaders in the organization.

Work to achieve strategic alignment in the organization through the leaders-as-teachers program. Leader-teachers are in pivotal positions to directly affect and encourage strategic alignment between the learning function and organizational goals and priorities. Whether serving as subject matter experts, providing input for the program development process, or serving directly in the classroom, opportunities abound to make this connection between strategy, learning, change, and business growth.

Break down organizational silos using the leaders-as-teachers program. Leaders who teach are in a great position to break down organizational silos. At BD, the idea of swapping and sharing or importing and exporting ideas, business knowledge, or learning resources is part of the culture. Call it what you will, this flow of information is vital to organizational health. And this easy flow of information and organizational learning is worth its weight in gold in today's competitive world. Barriers to knowledge, information, and learning resources can easily disable or at least handicap organizations. Learning and teaching organizations naturally create dozens of mechanisms for positive information and knowledge exchange and encourage continuous, spontaneous, and even serendipitous learning. This thinking encourages new ideas and creates fertile ground for business success.

Select leaders using Tichy's leadership model. Tichy's work is an outstanding starting point for a customized leadership selection process that will support a leaders-as-teachers program. Though each organization must create its own process and programs, Tichy's model and other related writings are a good base on which to build your leaders-as-teachers program.

The Influence of Bernard Haldane's Work

Although the work of Bernard Haldane does not specifically focus on the concept of leader as teachers, it has enabled me to draw important conceptual linkages to the practice of leaders as teachers. Haldane was an innovative behavioral scientist and a pioneer in the field of career development, career transition, and job search in the 1940s who developed breakthrough approaches in the area of personal strengths identification and utilization. He referred to this approach as Success Factor Analysis. This was one of the very early and successful methods for identifying and leveraging strengths. Variations of this approach remain very popular and useful today. Haldane suggested why people very frequently are willing to go out of their way to help and advise others when they are seeking advice. In doing so, he crystallized the fundamentals of what later would become many of the modern methods of job search, advice or information interviews, identification of transferable skills, networking, and other techniques in the field of career management and career transition.

At the heart of Haldane's work was the belief that people will share their expertise and help others for three primary, fairly universal reasons:

- ◆ Most people have goodwill and thus will help others with their career challenges in the workplace.
- ◆ Many people are proud of what they know or have accomplished, especially if they are regarded as experienced, competent, or expert by others.
- ◆ Many individuals' sense of self is enhanced when asked to share their experience, competence, or expertise with others.

Haldane's principles greatly influenced our thinking while setting up BD's leaders-as-teachers program. Here are the three major principles I derived from Haldane's work.

First, most people are naturally inclined to help others. Organizations considering a leaders-as-teachers program are often concerned about motivating a leader to teach. Haldane's early work in career management informed my point of view about how people's goodwill could be a contributing factor in the success of a leaders-as-teachers process. My personal experience with Haldane's work in the early 1980s helped me to appreciate the principle that *most people have goodwill and are willing to help others, especially with their career challenges and development.*

Second, most people are proud of their knowledge and accomplishments. People are naturally proud of their academic and career accomplishments. A leaders-as-teachers approach feeds this natural sense of pride when others see them as experienced, competent, and expert in their fields. All successful professionals and leaders have overcome many obstacles and faced their anxieties and fears. They have also leveraged their strengths, abilities, and talents to succeed. When teaching, coaching, or mentoring, leaders benefit from taking pride in the value of their experiences, career path, and accomplishments.

Third, sharing enhances a person's sense of self-worth. How do you feel when someone important to you asks you to demonstrate a skill or tell the story of how you overcame a difficulty? You likely feel a positive sense of self and appreciate that others respect you and what you have accomplished. You probably felt this as a child, and you likely have had the same reaction in your professional life. In the workplace, this motivating dynamic is vital for those in leadership roles to understand and apply.

These three principles are tremendous potential sources of teaching energy within organizations. They can be tapped in ways that enable experienced professionals, managers, and leaders to share their experience, leadership Teachable Points of View™, and expertise with others. There are vital and powerful points of leverage when these three principles derived from Haldane are combined with Tichy's pioneering leaders-as-teachers work.

The Influence of Tim Butler and Jim Waldroop

Similar to the work of Bernard Haldane, Tim Butler and Jim Waldroop's research and writing have not been focused specifically on the leaders-as-teachers approach. However, Butler and Waldroop's concepts are highly complementary with the work of Tichy and Haldane. They form

> **Leader's Perspective**
>
> John Hanson (executive vice president international, BD) says: From a personal learning perspective, there is a deep value in practicing leaders as teachers. Not only do you uncover talent hidden in the multiple layers in an organization, but it improves how you as a leader connect with individuals. Very often, in the informality of one-to-one discussions, not only can you provide coaching and mentoring; you can also gather feedback on what associates (and often their teams) are looking for in direction and motivation. This helps you think through future direction to bring the very best out of individuals and their respective teams with higher-energy-generating improved performance. One part of the process I insist on is that I always participate in the selection process for nominations to the leadership development courses to ensure that we are looking deep into the organization for future talent. It's amazing how often they can be overlooked in the hierarchy.

a motivational set of principles that have helped me to explain why many otherwise very busy leaders agree to and even desire to serve as leader-teachers. I have synthesized the work of these four leadership, career, and organizational experts to provide the primary motivational building blocks to support any organization wishing to establish a leaders-as-teachers process.

As social scientists and psychologists specializing in career development, Waldroop and Butler served as codirectors of the Career Development Center at the Harvard Business School. Butler remains in that university role, and along with Waldroop, has constructed evidence-based career assessment and development resources and methods. Their concept of *deeply embedded life interests* provided the link for me to the leaders-as-teachers approach. This concept, which refers to naturally occurring and emotionally driven passions, is explored and explained succinctly in their article "Job Sculpting: The Art of Retaining Your Best People," which noted that

> deeply embedded life interests are long-held, emotionally driven passions, intricately entwined with personality and thus born of an indeterminate mix of nature and nurture. Deeply embedded life interests do not determine what people are good at—they drive what kinds of activities make them happy. At work, that happiness often translates into commitment. It keeps people engaged, and it keeps them from quitting.... In our research, we found only eight deeply embedded life interests for people drawn to business careers.... Life interests start showing themselves in childhood and remain relatively stable throughout our lives, even though they may manifest themselves in different ways at different times.... Think of deeply embedded life interest as a geothermal pool of superheated water. It will rise to the surface in one place as a hot spring and in another as a geyser. But beneath the surface—at the core of the individual—the pool is constantly bubbling. Deeply embedded life interests always seem to find expression, even if a person has to change jobs—or careers—for that to happen. (Butler and Waldroop 1999, 145–46)

Build It and They Will Come

The concept of deeply embedded life interests reinforced our belief at BD University that if the leaders-as-teachers approach was established, *they would come*. We believed that a substantial number of leaders and associates would raise their hands to teach, in part, because of their particular deeply embedded life interest profile.

Butler and Waldroop outlined eight fundamental deeply embedded life interests that typically occur in different combinations and with different levels of intensity in individuals who choose to work in the business world. At BD, two combinations of these interests consistently aligned in those leaders who showed a desire to become a leader-teacher:

1. managing people and relationships, combined with counseling and mentoring
2. enterprise control (leading businesses), combined with influence through language and ideas.

Just as at BD, many leaders in many organizations have pent-up energy to teach, facilitate, coach, mentor, and express their points of view and to serve as role models. They utilize their *geothermal energy* to teach, coach, and mentor. Yet other leaders take time to write and partner with learning professionals about their life and work experiences, which helps immeasurably in course development.

Three Key Butler-Waldroop Concepts

BD adapted three key concepts derived from the research and writing of Butler and Waldroop. *First, deeply embedded life interests are powerful energy sources to be tapped.* Consciously or subconsciously, leaders and others strive to find positive venues for expression of their deeply embedded life interests. As noted above, Butler and Waldroop described this energy source beautifully: "Think of deeply embedded life interest as a geothermal pool of superheated water. It will rise to the surface in one place as a hot spring and in another as a geyser. But beneath the surface—at the core of the individual—the pool is constantly bubbling. Deeply embedded life interests always seem to find expression, even if a person has to change jobs—or careers—for that to happen."

For those with any level of desire to teach, their personal motivation will eventually win them over. The stored teaching, coaching, and mentoring energy of these leaders will find a natural and positive release that benefits others in the organization as well as themselves.

Second, create an organizational environment that supports deeply embedded life interests. Create an environment in your organization that supports those who have an interest in teaching. Make it safe, fun, rewarding, and with proper support and preparation, as easy as possible. Remove administrative burdens and barriers. Let one positive experience be the impetus for a second and third. Help leaders with positive teaching experiences recruit other leader-teachers. The pent up demand is always surprising.

Third, successfully combine the work of Tichy, Haldane, and Butler and Waldroop. Part of the basis for a successful leaders-as-teachers program is derived from applying principles developed by Tichy, Haldane, and Butler and Waldroop. By exploring these connections and taking advantage of the synergies, you can attract, engage, and retain your pool of leader-teachers. The resulting program will bring tremendous positive energy to your

Figure 4-1. A Simple Model Demonstrating How BD Used the Work of Organizational Experts to Build Its Leaders-as-Teachers Program

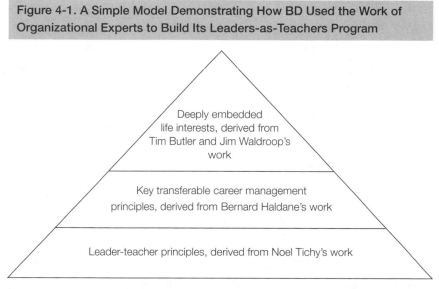

Note: This pyramid shows Tichy's work as a baseline support, and the work of Haldane and of Butler and Waldroop providing the overarching support based on several principles of human behavior.

organization and have a direct impact on business performance and organizational and leadership effectiveness. To help you visualize the synergies among the concepts presented in this chapter, figure 4-1 gives a conceptual model of their interrelation.

In the next chapter, key concepts from the work of John Kotter and Jim Collins are presented as support for the change process that must occur during the transition to a leaders-as-teachers approach.

◆ ◆ ◆

Implementation Activity 1: Apply Principles of Motivation and Human Nature to Attract Leader-Teachers

Step 1: For each of the following experts described in this chapter, what are several of the most important concepts or principles that you could use in your organization to recruit, engage, prepare, and utilize leader-teachers?

- ◆ Noel Tichy
- ◆ Bernard Haldane
- ◆ Tim Butler and Jim Waldroop.

Step 2: What are the specific steps you could take in your organization to apply these principles to recruit, engage, prepare, or utilize leaders to teach? You could use any one, a combination, or even all the principles you listed in step 1, to implement your actions.

List the principles you have chosen below:	Describe how you are going to apply each principle (individually or in combination) in your organizational setting:

Step 3: Describe the first one or two steps you are going to take and the date(s) by which you will take these steps to advance your organization's leader-teacher initiative.

Implementation Activity 2: Outline One of Your Leadership Teachable Points of View™

Leaders must develop their own personal Teachable Points of View™ and expect the same from other developing leaders. These points of view can be based on a wide range of issues, including individual and team effectiveness, business success, and values and ethically based conduct. However, leaders must understand the importance of consistency between their words and their actions, because not living up to your words is viewed as inconsistent or even hypocritical.

Step 1: Write in a sentence or two at the most the essence of what you strongly believe about one topic, such as what it takes to achieve business success, the importance of teamwork, work-related values, ethical behavior, fierce resolve and determination to achieve goals, demonstrating humility, being resourceful, or any other topic about which you have a deeply held leadership point of view.

Step 2: Do those with whom you work know how strongly felt this belief or leadership Teachable Point of View™ is for you—yes? no? maybe? If your answer is no or maybe, what actions can you take to strengthen how you communicate this point of view?

Step 3: Do others with whom you work see consistency between your actions/behavior and your words—yes? no? maybe? If your answer is no or maybe, what actions can you take to strengthen the consistency between your actions/behavior and your words?

Step 4 (optional): Many leaders like to convey their leadership Teachable Points of View™ in the form of a story, anecdote, or reference to a quotation or even a news or historical event. Using the leadership Teachable Point of View™ you selected above, outline the main elements of such a story or anecdote you could use to make your point a memorable one for others. Or is there a quotation, news story, or historical event that you might integrate into your leadership Teachable Point of View™?

Step 5: Practice telling your story or narrative to one or a few individuals whose opinion and feedback you trust and value. Then incorporate their suggestions for improvement.

Step 6: You are ready to use your leadership Teachable Point of View™ when the time and place is right for you.

Defying Gravity

Orchestrating a Leaders-as-Teachers Change Process

*I haven't failed—I've just found 10,000 ways
that don't work.*
—Thomas Edison

Success is never final.
—Winston Churchill

◆ ◆ ◆

What's Inside This Chapter?

Chapter 2 addressed the questions of *why* organizations choose to adopt the leaders-as-teachers approach and outlined six key reasons for implementing the program. Chapter 3 highlighted the dozens of ways leaders can participate in the leaders-as-teachers process in your organization. Chapter 4 described the behavioral and motivational drivers behind why leaders want to teach and how to utilize these human characteristics to attract senior executives and other leaders to serve as leader-teachers. This chapter addresses a change framework that overcomes resistance to change as the leaders-as-teachers program is introduced and incrementally expanded.

Essentially, leading change is like defying organizational gravity. One reason is that there is a natural tendency for organizations to reach their own comfortable "steady state" of functioning. Introducing change is hazardous duty and very challenging. Metaphorically, there are gravitational forces at work in all organizations that resist change and growth. In a twist of a law of physics, I like to say in organizational life, gravity never has a bad day, as was noted in chapter 2. Learning executives and other professionals involved in the change process must be skilled in leading organizational change and use this knowledge to navigate this often-difficult journey. I found the writings of two experts on organizational change and business success to be especially useful for BD's journey to introducing its leaders-as-teachers process: John Kotter and Jim Collins.

Kotter's Principles

The writings of John Kotter—the former Konosuke Matsushita Professor of Leadership at the Harvard Business School—have greatly influenced BD's approach to building, executing, and sustaining its leaders-as-teachers approach. His change model is particularly effective, because most people can easily understand its logical presentation and basis for implementation. In *Leading Change* (Kotter 1996) and *The Heart of Change* (Kotter and Cohen 2002), he describes eight immutable steps to effectively implement organizational planned change and outlines eight classic errors to avoid when leading changing. At BD, we took Kotter's principles and admonition to heart in our implementation. But before describing BD's change process experience, here is a listing and short description of Kotter's eight-stage change process and eight errors to avoid:

Kotter's Eight-Stage Change Process
1. Establish a sense of urgency:
    —Examine the market and competitive realities.
    —Identify and discuss crises, potential crises, or major opportunities.
2. Create the guiding coalition:
    —Put together a group with enough power to lead the change.
    —Get the group to work together like a team.

3. Develop a vision and strategy:
   —Create a vision to help direct the change effort.
   —Develop strategies for achieving that vision.
4. Communicate the change vision:
   —Use every vehicle possible to constantly communicate the new vision and strategies.
   —Have the guiding coalition role model the behavior expected of employees.
5. Empower broad-based action:
   —Get rid of obstacles.
   —Change systems or structures that undermine the change vision.
   —Encourage risk taking and nontraditional ideas, activities, and actions.
6. Generate short-term wins:
   —Plan for visible improvements in performance, or "wins."
   —Create those wins.
   —Visibly recognize and reward people who made the wins possible.
7. Consolidate the gains and produce more change:
   —Use increased credibility to change all systems, structures, and policies that don't fit together and don't fit the transformation vision.
   —Hire, promote, and develop people who can implement the change vision.
   —Reinvigorate the process with new projects, themes, and change agents.
8. Anchor new approaches in the culture:
   —Create better performance through customer- and productivity-oriented behavior, more and better leadership, and more effective management.
   —Articulate the connections between new behaviors and organizational success.
   —Develop means to ensure leadership development and succession (Kotter 1996, 21).

Kotter's Eight Change Errors to Avoid

1. Allowing too much complacency.
2. Failing to create a sufficiently powerful guiding coalition.
3. Underestimating the power of vision.
4. Undercommunicating the vision by a factor of 10 (100 or even 1,000).
5. Permitting obstacles to block the new vision.
6. Failing to create short-term wins.
7. Declaring victory too soon.
8. Neglecting to anchor changes firmly in the corporate culture (Kotter 1996, 4–16).

Implementing Change at BD

As noted, BD used Kotter's model and followed his advice to successfully implement the change to a leaders-as-teachers approach. What follows is an overview of BD's change activities based on Kotter's eight-stage change process. A follow-on sidebar reveals how BD managed to avoid the eight common errors of implementation.

Establishing a Sense of Urgency

The first aspect of establishing a sense of urgency is to examine market and competitive realities. In 2000, senior leaders at BD chartered a cross-functional team to develop specific recommendations with a clear sense of urgency. Members of this team benchmarked other companies. This facilitated the recognition that many other companies were addressing their learning and development needs in more effective and more consistent ways. The benchmarking also helped the senior leaders of the company to conclude that without additional focus and investment, BD would be at a competitive disadvantage from a talent management, leadership, and associate development perspective. The task team concluded that this could significantly affect the company's overall business capability and competitiveness.

The second aspect of establishing a sense of urgency is to identify and discuss crises, potential crises, or major opportunities. BD's initial examination of market forces—in addition to external benchmarking, internal surveys, focus groups, and other informal information-gathering methods—raised the issue that BD needed to focus on the development of associates' and leaders' careers at all levels. Senior leaders agreed with this assessment and committed to take advantage of the opportunity for company-wide improvement.

Creating the Guiding Coalition

The first aspect of creating the guiding coalition is to put together a group with enough power to lead the change. A cross-functional team worked with the senior learning and development leaders to develop specific recommendations that focused on how to address the identified concerns regarding leadership and associate development. This cross-functional task team developed a recommended vision, strategy, and related recommendations to establish a leaders-as-teachers process as the foundation of what would become BD University (BDU).

The second aspect of creating the guiding coalition is to get the group to work together like a team. The cross-functional team effort was so successful that it was the basis for the formation of the BDU Global Core Team. This global team represents the company's major businesses, geographic regions, and functions. Since 2000 this team of approximately 30 to 35 members has helped establish plans and priorities and has ensured worldwide implementation and resource sharing consistent with annual approved goals.

The BDU Global Core Team meets virtually every six weeks and in a live meeting every year or every other year. All members of this team are leader-teachers themselves, with the exception of several members who are primarily responsible for program coordination. Many are program champions on either a worldwide or local basis. Several members of this team lead one of five colleges within BDU. Most important, the team members directly support the leaders-as-teachers process from a recruitment, training, engagement, retention, and administrative perspective.

Developing a Vision and Strategy

The first aspect of developing a vision and strategy is to create a vision to help direct the change effort. The vision for the change effort was established during the formation of the guiding coalition. The vision was essentially to create a leaders-as-teachers-based learning and development process that was designed to help prepare professionals and especially leaders for current and future business challenges consistent with the company's growth strategies and goals.

The second aspect of developing a vision and strategy is to devise specific alternatives and plans and to examine the relative pros and cons involved as well as the consequences of achieving the vision. In doing this, the strengths and characteristics of the existing culture need to be examined. Will this culture support or strongly resist change? Can the existing culture be leveraged for positive change, or will every step be the equivalent of an organizational dogfight? There is an expression that "culture eats strategy for lunch." Culture needs to be deeply understood, not underestimated, and then converted into an important lever for change.

The BDU staff and the Global Core Team update strategies and modify the annual plan during the year as needed. One key element of each annual plan is the continuous strengthening of the leaders-as-teachers process. In doing this, current and projected business conditions are analyzed. Cultures and business conditions are dynamic, and regular assessments determine what elements of the corporate university, its curricula, and the leaders-as-teachers process will be emphasized, expanded, modified, or reduced for a period of time. These plans are reviewed and approved or modified with input from the company's top human resources team and subsequently from its senior executive team.

Communicating the Change Vision

The first aspect of communicating the change vision is to use every vehicle possible to constantly communicate the new vision and strategies. BD used multiple vehicles to communicate its new vision, but face-to-face interactions were the most powerful. Face-to-face meetings conveyed the importance of the effort and the energy driving the initiative more effectively whether these interactions happened in large departmental meetings, small team meetings, or individual meetings. As always, the involved leaders and coaches were the most effective proponents of the organizational change.

The second aspect of communicating the change vision is to ensure that the guiding coalition models the behavior expected of employees. In addition to the role of the BDU Global Core Team, almost all members of the company's leadership team are leader-teachers. Most important, the members of the office of the CEO, composed of the five top executives of the company, are active role models for leader-teacher values— including Ed Ludwig, who is BD's chairman and CEO.

Empowering Broad-Based Action

Empowering broad-based action entails getting rid of obstacles; changing systems or structures that undermine the change vision; and encouraging risk taking and nontraditional ideas, activities, and actions. Well more than 500 leaders and professionals have taught throughout the world at BD. This has required changing mental models and previous practices, ensuring extensive preparation, reducing administrative obstacles, and providing recognition for leader-teachers. The leaders-as-teachers process takes advantage of certain aspects of the company's preexisting culture, but the change has required new individual and organizational risk taking that BD has strongly supported from the beginning.

Generating Short-Term Wins

The first aspect of generating short-term wins is to plan for visible improvements in performance—these are initial short-term wins. Frequently, these are precedent-setting events. They are new and different. They begin to change the status quo. After establishing the first program with a few leader-teachers, follow-on programs were established in a methodical and visible manner. Each leader-teacher identified was either a senior leader or an individual with a "high influential" profile who helped to recruit other leader-teachers. These initial leaders created quick and sustained positive organizational "buzz." These early actions are examples of the "see-feel-act" change paradigm that Kotter presents in *The Heart of Change*, pointing out that people are much more ready to change when they see or experience something with real meaning. Being taught by respected leaders is often a compelling experience that frequently influences others to join the process. When the organizational culture increasingly supports these teaching and coaching practices, Butler and Waldroop's dynamic of natural or deeply embedded life interests in the areas of teaching, facilitation, and coaching is provided with a receptive venue.

The second aspect of generating short-term wins is to create the next and then the following wins. At BD, the theme of ensuring that every teaching-learning experience is valuable and has business and personal benefits drove every program offered. Staying focused on high expectations helped recruit and engage other leader-teachers who shared that value. The culture was experiencing the initial signs of change.

The third aspect of generating short-term wins is to visibly recognize and reward people who make the wins possible. BD ensured that public and private recognition practices were in place. These practices included recognition lunches, highlighting successes in organizational announcements, personal thank-you notes, and acts as simple as the distribution and wearing of BDU leader-teacher shirts and blouses. These and other practices reinforced the giving of one's self as a leader-teacher. They also helped build a sense of pride in the role. In addition, BD ensured that participation in the program was part of human resources planning, including consideration as part of succession planning.

Leader's Perspective

Deborah Wijnberg (global human resources leader/talent management at BD) says: One of the things that always amazes me about the impact of the leaders-as-teachers methodology is how much true learning and change occurs when leaders are asked to teach others. At BD, it was fascinating to experience how leadership vocabulary and behavior actually evolved simply because leaders spent time teaching concepts and new approaches. For example, eight years ago, when the concepts around John Kotter's change management methodology were first introduced, it was quite new to most leaders. Spring ahead four years, and when an organizational change needs to occur in the company, as a natural part of the planning process for that change, one hears leaders discussing how they will "create a sense of urgency," "establish a guiding coalition," and the like. This type of thing happens all around the world at BD today!

Consolidating Gains and Producing More Change

The first aspect of consolidating gains and producing more change is to use increased credibility to change all systems, structures, and policies that do not fit the transformation vision. BD has examined and changed workflows and implemented a variety of continuous improvement processes to ensure the effectiveness and efficiency of the leaders-as-teachers process.

The second aspect of consolidating gains and producing more change is to hire, promote, and develop people who can implement the change vision. BD established a small but very highly qualified BDU and talent management team, which regularly recruited new or different BDU Global Core Team members along with hundreds of highly effective leader-teachers.

The third aspect of consolidating gains and producing more change is to reinvigorate the process with new projects, themes, and change agents. As the leaders-as-teachers approach grew, new initiatives were undertaken for further progressive growth and improvement. Experienced leader-teachers were provided with opportunities to modify, reduce, or expand their teaching responsibilities. Meanwhile, a pipeline of interested but often less experienced leader-teachers was given new opportunities, and the abilities of these leader-teachers were stretched through progressive teaching roles.

Anchoring New Approaches in the Culture

At BD, the leaders-as-teachers process anchored the new approaches to learning, communications, and values transmission in the company's culture. It contributed to better performance, better leadership, and more effective management practices. Great care was taken to stay close to our internal customers while achieving alignment with business strategies and goals. A sampling of these approaches included regular organizational needs and information sensing, analyzing voice-of-the-customer data, and inclusion of the leader-teacher approach in strategic planning and in-company communication vehicles. Governance and ongoing approval of the leaders-as-teachers program include high visibility with senior leaders, meetings, presentations, one-to-one discussions, and coteaching with many of these same executives. Beginning in 2000, these were some of the communication methods used in a new way of doing business to establish and execute the learning and talent development agenda. In addition, the process of identifying well-qualified and highly engaged leader-teachers has become a reliable way to help develop new organizational leaders and a key part of the growth strategy at BD.

◆ ◆ ◆

How BD Managed to Avoid the Eight Errors of Leading Change

Error 1: Allowing too much complacency. Strategy for avoiding: The leaders-as-teachers process at BD is very active and highly visible across the globe. Achieving high-impact results, the involvement of leaders at all levels, modeling continuous improvement, and striving for sustainability are hallmarks.

Error 2: Failing to create a sufficiently powerful guiding coalition. Strategy for avoiding: The BDU Global Core Team, more than 500 leader-teachers, and consistent senior-level executive dialogue, support, and involvement are all in place to prevent this error from occurring.

Error 3: Underestimating the power of vision. Strategy for avoiding: At BD, vision and strategy for the program is addressed annually or biannually as part of BD University's ongoing leaders-as-teachers strategic plan. We also communicate this plan and vision to various supporting BD guiding coalitions and constituencies and seek input from them on the plan. This often requires negotiations to ensure that resources are allocated and balanced with other initiatives for leadership development and talent management.

Error 4: Undercommunicating the vision by a factor of 10 (100 or even 1,000). Strategy for avoiding: (1) having the primary stakeholders and guiding coalitions directly involved in the key elements of the leaders-as-teachers process; (2) and having these same groups serve as primary vehicles for the vision and strategy as well as other important aspects of the leaders-as-teachers process.

Error 5: Permitting obstacles to block the new vision. Strategy for avoiding: This error is mitigated by a culture of excellence and continuous improvement. The right people are designated to be leaders as teachers, process champions, and program champions. There is a culture characterized by a bias for action, that is results oriented, and that has a sense of urgency in addressing challenges, obstacles, and problems preventively, rapidly, and effectively.

Error 6: Failing to create short-term wins. Strategy for avoiding: The leaders-as-teachers process at BD is designed to regularly achieve short-term wins and then incrementally leverage these wins to build momentum for more or greater wins. I refer to this as "little mo to big mo." You cannot achieve "big mo" until you have "little mo." In Collins's terms, this is effecting the first turn of a flywheel and then progressively achieving a full flywheel effect. A typical example is building a worldwide cohort of experienced leader-teachers for a designated program when initially only two or three leader-teachers were identified to launch the program. This incremental, progressive approach is a low- to medium-risk, high-potential change process. It is the antithesis of the big-bang, high-visibility, high-risk approach to change and the introduction of new programs and processes taken by some organizations.

Error 7: Declaring victory too soon. Strategy for avoiding: It was not until the second or third year of the worldwide implementation of the leaders-as-teachers approach at BD that I was willing to concede that significant and potentially sustainable progress was being made. I would regularly profess the virtues of underpromising and overdelivering on stakeholders' expectations. For imaginative and visual impact, I would often use a child/human development metaphor to describe where I thought we were and where we would need to be in the next phase of the leaders-as-teachers change process. I would say things like "I believe we are leaving infancy. We are beginning to enter toddlerhood, where we are beginning to take some cautious but independent steps." Or, "We are leaving adolescence, but there is a long way to go before we have a mature process."

Error 8: Neglecting to anchor changes firmly in the corporate culture. Strategy for avoiding: The leaders-as-teachers process at BD is now in its ninth year. It is thriving around the world primarily because of the way it continues to be part of the business's growth engine and the way it is embedded in the corporate-wide culture and in many business, geographic, and functional subcultures.

◆ ◆ ◆

The description in the sidebar represents BD's efforts to implement its leaders-as-teachers program following Kotter's model. For help with your own initiative, see the implementation exercise at the end of this chapter.

◆ ◆ ◆

Major points for leaders-as-teachers implementing Kotter's insights:

◆ Change is very hard. It is essential to utilize an organizational change model when implementing a leaders-as-teachers process in an organization.

◆ The use of a change model is not only essential to jump start a leaders-as-teachers approach to organizational teaching and learning, but it is equally important to progressively build and sustain the model.

◆ In using an organizational planned change process to start and implement a leaders-as-teachers approach, it is important to know what steps to take and in what order. It is also vital to know how to avoid the errors that can derail the effort.

◆ ◆ ◆

Kotter's change principles were a major source of the change process that helped drive BD's implementation of the leaders-as-teachers approach. We have revisited each of the eight steps described above many times to reinforce concepts or prevent or solve problems. Those championing the leaders-as-teachers process across the enterprise took seriously Kotter's admonitions to not declare victory too early, and Kotter's warnings continue to ring true. The skillful deployment of an organizational planned change process requires work and ongoing involvement from many people. However, the rewards have far exceeded the organization's rigorous effort and investment.

The Influence of Jim Collins's Business and Change Principles

Jim Collins's influence on how companies think about leadership, leadership development, business growth, change leadership, and other topics essential to the long-term health of organizations is well known. His concepts have had a profound impact on thousands of organizations and leaders in for-profit, not-for-profit, and academic institutions. Though Collins's work does not directly address implementing a leaders-as-teachers process, BD drew valuable insights derived from his work in both the startup phase of the project and in the operation of the program as it exists today. Ed Ludwig—BD's chairman and CEO—had already embraced many of Collins's principles as part of his leadership philosophy. In addition, Collins had consulted with Ludwig and his predecessor, Clateo Castellini, on several occasions beginning in the middle to late 1990s. And Collins spoke to more than 150 of BD's top leaders at a global leadership meeting in 1998.

Strength from Collins's Principles

Given this history, it is not surprising that BD selected principles from Collins's two books, *Built to Last* and *Good to Great*, to help guide the implementation of its leaders-as-teachers program. Ten of these principles were particularly helpful in establishing and sustaining the program:

1. Clock building, not time telling.
2. No "tyranny of the or" (embrace the "genius of the and").
3. Preserve the core/stimulate progress.
4. Big hairy audacious goals.
5. Good is the enemy of great.
6. Level 5 leadership.
7. First who, ... then what.
8. Confront the brutal facts (never lose faith).
9. A culture of discipline.
10. The flywheel and doom loop.

The first four of these principles are described in *Built to Last* (Collins and Porras 1994). Here is an explanatory passage taken directly from the book for each of these principles:

1. *Clock building, not time telling:* "Having a great idea or being a charismatic visionary leader is 'time telling'; building a company that can prosper far beyond the presence of any single leader and through multiple product life cycles is 'clock building'" (p. 23).

2. *No "tyranny of the or" (embrace the "genius of the and"):* "The 'tyranny of the *or*' pushes people to believe that things must be either A *or* B, but not both. It makes such proclamations as 'You can have change *or* stability,' 'You can be conservative *or* bold,' 'You can have low cost *or* high quality,' and 'You can invest for the future *or* do well in the short term.' Instead of being oppressed by the 'tyranny of the *or*,' highly visionary companies liberate themselves with the 'genius of the *and*'— the ability to embrace both extremes of a number of dimensions at the same time. Instead of choosing between A *or* B, they figure out a way to have both A *and* B: A relatively fixed core ideology *and* vigorous change and movement; conservatism around the core *and* bold, committing, risky moves; the selection of managers steeped in the core *and* the selection of managers who induce change; ideological control *and* operational autonomy; philosophical, visionary, futuristic *and* superb daily execution, 'nuts and bolts'" (pp. 43–44).

3. *Preserve the core/stimulate progress:* Understand the dynamic interplay between core ideology and the drive for progress: core ideology drives for progress; provides continuity and stability; urges continual change; relatively fixed stake in the ground impels constant movement; limits possibilities and directions; expands possibilities and directions (adapted from p. 85).

4. *Big hairy audacious goals (BHAGs):* "A true BHAG is clear and compelling and serves as a unifying focal point of effort—often creating immense team spirit" (p. 94). "It's not just the presence of a goal that stimulates progress; it is also the level of commitment to the goal. Indeed, a goal cannot be classified as a BHAG without a high level of commitment to the goal" (p. 100).

The last six of these principles are described in *Good to Great* (Collins 2002). Here is an explanatory passage taken directly from the book for each of these principles:

5. *Good is the enemy of great:* "And that is one of the key reasons why we have so little that becomes great" (p. 1).

6. *Level 5 leadership:* "We were surprised, shocked really, to discover the type of leadership required for turning a good company into a great one.... a paradoxical blend of personal humility and professional will" (p. 13).

7. *First who, ... then what:* "We expected that the good-to-great leaders would begin by setting a new vision and strategy. We found instead that they first got the right people on the bus, the wrong people off the bus, and the right people in the right seats—and then they figured out where to drive it. The old adage 'People are your most important asset' turns out to be wrong. People are not your most important asset. The right people are" (p. 130).

8. *Confront the brutal facts (never lose faith):* "Every good-to-great company embraced what we came to call the Stockdale Paradox: You must maintain unwavering faith that you can and will prevail in the end, regardless of the difficulties, *and* at the same time have the discipline to confront the most brutal facts of your current reality, whatever they might be" (p. 130).

9. *A culture of discipline:* "All companies have a culture, some companies have discipline, but few companies have a culture of discipline. When you have disciplined people, you don't need hierarchy. When you have disciplined thought, you don't need bureaucracy. When you have disciplined action, you don't need excessive controls. When you combine a culture of discipline with an ethic of entrepreneurship, you get the magical alchemy of great performance" (p. 130).

10. *The flywheel and doom loop:* "No matter how dramatic the end result, the good-to-great transformations never happened in one fell swoop. There was no single defining action, no grand program, no one killer innovation, no solitary lucky break, no miracle moment. Rather, the process resembled relentlessly pushing a giant heavy flywheel in one direction, turn upon turn, building momentum until a point of breakthrough, and beyond" (p. 14).

Applying Collins's Principles

A full reading of both the classic business books *Built to Last* and *Good to Great* is not necessary to understand the profound implications of following the sage wisdom included in the quotations presented above. Collins's work can provide the basic framework for any organization to improve. In the implementation of BD's leaders-as-teachers program, the takeaways were hugely important for ultimate success. Let's consider the major application points BD derived from Collins's work.

As described above, BD's leaders had a vision of leaders serving as teachers. However, when the right leaders are in place, everything else follows. The leaders-as-teachers process begins primarily with the "who," not the "what." In both the selection of the professional staff that spearhead the leaders-as-teachers process, as well as the selection of the initial and subsequent cadres of leaders who teach, everything builds from "the who." The selection of the right leaders who drive the process, and those who are the initial teaching role models, is a high indicator for success over time. These same individuals become the ones who develop the great ideas for growth and also embed the practices so deeply in the organization's culture that the sustainability of the approach results.

Building a leaders-as-teachers process that is sustainable—that will thrive and survive over time—requires building from basics, setting deep and sound foundations, and thoroughly aligning the process with the organization's strategies, business goals, and values. It also includes continuously improving everything involved in the leaders-as-teachers process. In Collins's terms, this is "clock building," and it is also an important example of his principle of "good is the enemy of great."

As you plan your leaders-as-teachers approach, a vital clock-building strategy is to engineer your process for the long term while jump-starting it with "quick wins"—which are important to begin to build momentum. This is best done by using inch-by-inch, step-by-step progressions. The first steps could be to have one or two leaders teach one module or one program together, possibly along with a learning and development professional. Initially, achieve one program success, then a second and a third. Energy and momentum are built through successive wins. One success begets the next and then the next. These are the first, slow turns of what could eventually become a powerful flywheel.

Utilizing Collins's concept of "the genius of the and" requires an organization and its leaders to

- maintain their very busy work-related calendars *and* embrace teaching and coaching as part of their leadership roles
- continue to utilize the best of what works in their learning and development function *and* complement these existing actions with the practice of leaders serving as teachers
- build on the organization's core strategies and plans *and* stimulate business growth through leadership development and learning
- achieve quick wins *and* build for sustainability.

In at least one part of your organization, set a goal, a big goal—possibly even a big, hairy, audacious goal—of achieving a comprehensive, leaders-as-teachers process that will be up and running within 12 to 24—or "xyz"—months. Strive to establish the leadership commitment to make it happen.

Good is the enemy of great. Whether your effort is small or large scale, do not settle for anything less than achieving excellence in every aspect of the process in your organization. Ensure that nothing but the highest-quality planning and execution is involved in program content, leader-teacher preparation, and the actual teaching by leaders. Left to its own devices, good will be the enemy of great in the leader-teacher domain as it is in other aspects of business and organizational life.

Personal leadership agendas should never interfere with the implementation of the leaders-as-teachers process. Quite to the contrary, the leader(s) who drive the process and the leaders who teach in it best serve the organization by striving to consistently demonstrate level 5 leadership—that is, the will and fierce resolve for great results coupled with humility.

Leading the change process of implementing the leaders-as-teachers approach is hard work—very hard work. Accept the reality of where your organization is as a starting point (the brutal facts), but never lose faith that you will make progress and contribute in significant ways to your business and organization.

Senior-Level Involvement Is the Key to Defying Gravity

Even with the backing of well-researched change models and the application of principles from renowned business and organizational experts, change and success are elusive without the full support of senior management. At BD, the sense of urgency, guidance, support, and active involvement from Ed Ludwig and his leadership team are key elements of BD's leaders-as-teachers program success. Senior leadership's continued direct involvement and counsel have ensured strategic and goal alignment and helped BDU offer practical, reality-based programs. Figure 5-1 is a simple way to represent all the change, motivational, and implementation factors discussed thus far in chapter 4 and this chapter. The illustration shows the interdependence of all external and internal factors that drove BD's successful leaders-as-teachers program implementation.

Six Additional Factors That Contributed to Implementation Success

The final section of this chapter briefly examines five additional factors that contributed to the implementation success at BD and can be very useful in your organization:

- Senior leader and high-influencer involvement (not just support) and positive peer influence.
- Organizational buzz and branding.
- Every day is showtime.
- Going to the light.
- Little mo (momentum) leads to big mo.
- Links to talent management processes.

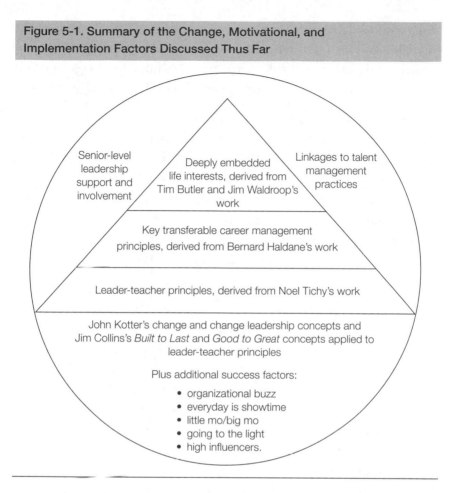

Figure 5-1. Summary of the Change, Motivational, and Implementation Factors Discussed Thus Far

Senior-level leadership support and involvement

Deeply embedded life interests, derived from Tim Butler and Jim Waldroop's work

Linkages to talent management practices

Key transferable career management principles, derived from Bernard Haldane's work

Leader-teacher principles, derived from Noel Tichy's work

John Kotter's change and change leadership concepts and Jim Collins's *Built to Last* and *Good to Great* concepts applied to leader-teacher principles

Plus additional success factors:

- organizational buzz
- everyday is showtime
- little mo/big mo
- going to the light
- high influencers.

As mentioned above, senior leadership involvement and support is key to success. Support can come in different forms, including financial support and written and verbal support (supportive messages at the right places and at the right time). However, what truly ignites and sustains the process is direct involvement by senior executives and other key leaders. Actions do speak louder than words.

Senior Leaders and High Influencers

Every business and organization has individuals who are capable of positively or negatively influencing the thinking and actions of other leaders and associates. These are individuals with strong influence management capability and are often referred to as *high influencers*. Though they may come from the executive ranks, very often high influencers can be found in middle management and in other important roles.

Frequently, high influencers are executives in key roles. However, many high influencers are seasoned professionals and are sometimes called "hi-pros." Typically, these leaders have high integrity and great know-how that they have developed over long periods of time. These individuals influence a lot of what is embraced or what is rejected in team and organizational settings. Some high influencers serve the role of organizational gatekeepers, whose support can provide access and availability to the executives, leaders, and managers with whom they work.

Most high influencers model what is really important, acceptable, or valued through their actions and behaviors. High influencers frequently have earned the respect of others and have access to the organizational airwaves. When they speak and act, others watch, listen, and often follow. Their role modeling and actions have a large ripple effect in their organizations. Winning over both senior leaders and these high influencers is key to program success. Their support and direct involvement are crucial because they are a form of positive peer influence.

Organizational Buzz

These organizational high influencers are also powerful because they help to create organizational buzz or the way the leaders-as-teachers process is viewed and talked about by others. If you gain their trust and engage them as leader-teachers or simply as active supporters of the approach, you will increase your likelihood of recruiting other leader-teachers whom you will want to have teach and whom others will respect in the classroom. (See the implementation activity at the end of this chapter to help you identify and gain support for these high influencers.)

Senior leaders and other high influencers frequently are factors in achieving the necessary leverage that can convert your efforts from quick wins into sustained adoption. When this type of positive peer influence begins to have its effect, a type of organizational branding can occur. At BD, this began to happen in the first six to nine months of 2000 as the first wave of BDU programs was introduced. Each of these programs was cotaught by carefully selected leaders and others whose influence in the organization was very high. The selection of these individuals was very deliberate. Encouraging and upbeat organizational buzz had begun and could be heard in many parts of the organization.

Every Day Is Showtime

Just like a Broadway show when the curtain goes up, each member of the audience develops first impressions of the show in seconds and long-lasting impressions in the minutes that follow. In part, this is the way the show's brand image is formed and the way it is described in the buzz by its customers and constituencies. In similar ways, this is how initial and long-lasting impressions of the leaders-as-teachers brand is formed. Every program, each teaching-learning opportunity, every planning and program design meeting, and every interaction makes a difference in the minds of others.

One of the best ways to build a positive brand image and stimulate positive hallway buzz for the leaders-as-teachers process in your organization is to value every opportunity as a showtime moment. The effectiveness of every program, of every planning and program design meeting, and of every type of interaction with others will contribute to the perceived value and potential business impact of the leaders-as-teachers brand. At BD, it was always showtime when leaders as teachers was the topic of conversations or meetings. Every moment is showtime—an opportunity to manage perceptions, the brand, and the buzz.

Going to the Light/Little Mo and Big Mo

"Going to the light" is an important concept for change leadership that I coined earlier in my career when I realized the futility of focusing too much attention on resistors while I was leading change efforts. "Light" is organizational energy and, in particular, the energy emanating from certain people and parts of an organization. At BD, we started using the phrase "going to the light" in 2000, when we concluded that some part of the organization seemed initially apathetic, disinterested, or resistant to the early stages of change to a leaders-as-teachers approach. Our team committed to establishing little mo (momentum) in those parts of the organization that were receptive to learning and development and specifically to engage one or more of their leaders to serve as teachers. These individuals became the company's leader-teacher pioneers or early adopters.

The early introduction of the leaders-as-teachers approach at BD was far from the Collins flywheel concept. But getting the wheel to turn, no matter how slowly, was considered a victory for future faster turns. Little mo had begun to form. This change principle is simple. As was stated above, you can't achieve big mo (momentum) until you have established little mo in one or more locations in your organization. The reality is that some parts of your organization are not ready for change, so finding leaders in these parts of the organization will be difficult. Find pockets of energy in the organization where experimentation and risk taking are higher and where you detect an early, sometimes immediate, interest in the concept of leaders teaching, developing, and coaching other leaders and associates. Convert little mo into big mo there, and use this as a temporary base camp. Then look for the light again in another part of the organization.

Links to Talent Management Processes

Finally, linking the leaders-as-teachers process to your organization's talent management processes is valuable and effective in encouraging change. It also is essential for short- and long-term sustainability. Consider these examples from BD's experience. Each practice has helped to further embed the leaders-as-teachers process in the business and its culture. Clearly, leader-teachers build their internal networks and expand their career possibilities by being part of leader-teacher communities of practice:

- ◆ Demonstrating a track record of talent development including teaching, coaching, and exporting talent to other parts of the company is one criterion used in identifying high-potential talent in the organization.
- ◆ The Individual Talent Profile or HR Planning Profile is a one-to two-page management document that is used in most large

organizations. At BD, these documents are updated annually by BD executives, managers, and professionals. Individuals update their own profiles, which require next-level electronic approval to be finalized. The HR Planning Profiles are regularly used during succession and talent planning reviews by senior leaders as they periodically review their organization. On an annual basis, these talent reviews roll up to BD's chairman and CEO. Several years after BD began to implement its leaders-as-teachers process, the chairman and CEO said he wanted to know what leaders were teaching and who was planning to teach. Since 2003, two small boxes have appeared on the profile: "Check the first box if you have taught in BDU during the previous two years. Check the second box if you plan to teach during the next year." This is visibility with both incentive and expectation built in.

♦ Talent development is part of the performance management process for managers and leaders.

♦ BD's leaders-as-teachers process is one of the elements embedded in BD's talent brand image. The company wants to communicate that it embraces talent development and that leader-teachers are the backbone of the teaching and learning process in the company.

♦ As mentioned above, when an internal promotion occurs involving a professional or leader who teaches, it is not uncommon for the individual's leader-teacher responsibilities (for example, is a faculty member for the Leadership Development and Advanced Leadership programs) to be cited in the organizational announcement of the individual's promotion.

♦ ♦ ♦

Implementation Activity 1: Using a Change Leadership Model to Begin a Leaders-as-Teachers Process

Step 1: Using the change leadership model described above, or any other change framework in which you have confidence, outline the primary, step-by-step actions you could take to help in successfully implementing a leaders-as-teachers process in your organization.

Step 2: Identify what steps in your plan are most likely to be successful or, for any number of reasons, easier to implement in your organization.

Step 3: What elements of your change plan do you feel are less likely to be successful or will be more difficult to implement in your organization?

Step 4: For each element you identify in step 3, you will need to move your planning into either a preventive or troubleshooting mode. What steps do you need to take or what resources are required to be mobilized to prevent or mitigate issues in implementing a leaders-as-teachers process in your organization? Whose support do you need to gain?

Step 5: What are the initial actions you will take to help ensure the success of your leaders-as-teachers implementation?

Implementation Activity 2: Identifying and Gaining the Support of High Influencers

Step 1: List three to five—or more, if you wish—high influencers in your organization whose support and involvement is important for the success of the leaders-as-teachers process in your organization.

Step 2: What do you need to do to win the support of each person you identified in step 1? List your actions for each individual.

Chapter 6

Help Your Leaders Be Stars

The Four Principles for Recruiting and Preparing Leaders to Teach

Luck favors the prepared mind.
—Louis Pasteur

◆ ◆ ◆

What's Inside This Chapter?

Chapters 1 though 3 explored the strategic and organizational benefits of a leaders-as-teachers approach and demonstrated the many ways leaders may participate. Chapters 4 and 5 explored theories and strategies that encourage leaders-as-teachers participation and discussed ways to bring about the necessary organizational change that nurtures and supports the process. This chapter shows you concrete ways to recruit and prepare top-notch leader-teachers based on four overarching principles:

♦ Match teaching assignments with the leader's background, expertise, responsibilities, and interests.
♦ Make sure leaders are well prepared to teach.
♦ Leaders should teach at the level of their confidence and effectiveness.
♦ Use active teaching and training methods in program design.

◆ ◆ ◆

Every teaching engagement is showtime for leader-teachers, for the students who learn from them, and for the corporate university or learning function that sponsors the program. Broadway shows are only as good as the script, the choreography, and the selection and the preparation of their casts. The same is true for training programs and other learning opportunities that are taught or facilitated by leader-teachers.

When I speak with other learning leaders and business executives about their teaching successes and disappointments, four overarching principles emerge. These four principles are the foundation of recruiting and selecting a pool of leader-teachers. Let's look at each principle.

Principle 1: Match Teaching Assignments with the Leader's Background, Expertise, Responsibilities, and Interests

Collins's adage—"First who, then what"—is a valuable guidepost when recruiting and matching leaders to programs. First, recruit the right leaders. Second, match leaders to programs that they are excited to teach. Finally, help the leaders to be prepared and confident when they teach. Here are seven tips for encouraging leader-teachers to volunteer. Leaders will volunteer to teach if they are

1. encouraged and recognized to teach by the organization's culture.
2. able to share what they know, including their leadership Teachable Points of View™.
3. confident that their contribution will build individual and organizational capability and add business value.
4. supported by learning and development professionals in the preparation period in advance of actually teaching.
5. confident that they will be successful when they teach.
6. able to enjoy themselves and take pride in their contribution. This condition is directly associated with matched interests, backgrounds, experience, and capabilities.
7. comfortable with the total amount of time necessary to prepare and to teach.

My experience is that these seven elements are necessary regardless of whether executives are individually recruited for a specific teaching assignment or groups of leaders are encouraged to volunteer to teach in one or more programs. Meeting all seven conditions is not always necessary for success, because some conditions have greater value to the individual than others. But meeting as many conditions as possible is an important determining factor for success. Here are two other ways to ensure program and leader-teacher match.

First, invite key leaders to teach or coteach a specific program. Use this approach when you wish to control who will teach in a clearly identified program. If you can get the CEO and other senior executive leaders involved, the high-profile support will help jump-start a leaders-as-teachers program and provide a positive role model for other potential leader-teachers. More important, high-level involvement sets a cultural and expectation tone from the top. Many organizations have one or more programs that fall into this category with high-end, flagship, leadership development experiences provided by CEOs, presidents, general managers, or those who lead local, national, or global functions, such as manufacturing, medical affairs, supply chain, law, or human resources.

Attendance for these high-end programs is often restricted based on specific criteria. The criteria are usually linked to current and projected leadership responsibilities or leadership potential and require top leaders and functional experts to serve as faculty. A real plus of these programs is that the experience and personal maturity of these leaders provide opportunity for leadership Teachable Points of View™. Inviting these leaders builds leader-teacher bench strength and helps build strong, positive linkages for the program. Most important, these leaders are honored to be asked because it is recognition of their value to the organization and will likely see their contribution as a way to add business value to the organization.

You can involve these senior leaders by

♦ pairing senior leaders with less senior leaders and leader-teachers. This connection builds a natural flow of teaching talent from one generation of a program to the next. It also creates the conditions for mentoring relationships to form. This approach also facilitates the preparation and learning process of leader-teachers, another condition for success, by allowing for carefully designed teaching progressions and the stretching of one's teaching comfort zone.

◆ inviting seasoned leaders and functional leaders to serve as faculty on programs with a specific focus. Use this approach for topics, such as finance for nonfinancial managers, lean Six Sigma, and business development. The benefits include building long-term program strength and mentoring possibilities.

The second way to ensure program and leader-teacher match is to recruit and develop pools of leader-teachers through personal interaction. Often, leader-teachers are attracted to the process as a result of their participation in a leader-led program. The inspiration to participate comes as a desire to share their Teachable Points of View™ and professional experiences and to exercise deeply embedded life interests involving teaching, coaching, and mentoring. This dynamic is very common and is enhanced when another respected leader-teacher asks a leader to teach. Often, the simple act of asking who might be interested in teaching a particular program invariably generates more interest than you expect.

The power of classroom modeling and enthusiasm is consistent in three ways with the conditions for the recruitment of leader-teachers, as noted above. The first is the personal impact and perception of value that participants experience as a result of a well-taught and -facilitated program. The second is a desire and willingness by participants to pass their valuable learning on to others, a dynamic similar to what Haldane found in career interactions in the 1940s, as was noted in chapter 4. The third factor is the powerful energy generated as a result of the influence of positive leader-teacher role models in the classroom or in other learning and developmental environments.

Here are some tips on building a slate of teachers. Once you build a little bit of momentum and gain some traction for the leaders-as-teachers approach, your pool of leader-teachers volunteering to teach will begin to grow naturally. Some deliberate prodding also helps at times. You may have to find program-specific "certified" leader-teachers to fill some spots, but the interest is surprising.

This volunteer approach works best when specific program offerings are posted on a schedule of three, six, or 12 months ahead. Usually, your most senior executives are not needed to teach major portions of regularly scheduled midlevel programs. You probably will want to pick and carefully choose which programs you will ask these executives to teach. Small, program-specific, train-the-trainer groups of approximately five to 12 individuals usually serve as the primary means to orient and train leader-teachers for these types of teaching roles:

- ◆ Recruit leader-teachers here, there, everywhere. Remarkably, leader-teachers are often found in places you least expect. I have recruited leader-teachers in boardrooms, classrooms, offices, hallways, the fitness center and locker room, in cafeteria lines, on airplanes, and at staff and team meetings. The point is to be a constant advocate for your program.
- ◆ Match the right leader to the right program and teaching assignments. It just makes great sense to take advantage of the knowledge leaders have gained through their years of experience and academic training. In addition, consider that every leader has individual preferences, learning styles, and personal interests. Help leaders discover their own teaching preparation style as they prepare to teach specific programs (see the sidebar for examples).

With respect to the idea of recruiting everywhere, one of my favorite recruiting stories of a leader-teacher actually occurred during a fire drill in 2004. There was a particular leader I had my recruiting eye on for some time but had experienced difficulty meeting with because of calendar conflicts. One early, bright spring day the company held one of its fire drills. Everyone at our corporate campus dutifully left his or her office and building when the signals sounded to begin the fire drill. It turned out to be a fortuitous moment. This leader and I caught up with each other while standing on the damp lawn outside our building. Ten minutes later, with dew on both of our shoes, I had the agreement that I was looking for. My colleague had agreed to join a new cohort to teach a program that she had participated in about a month and a half earlier.

◆ ◆ ◆

Ensuring an Effective Program-Leader Match

The following are examples of questions you can use when trying to ensure an effective match between a leader's background, learning style, current responsibilities, teaching interests, and the type of program content he or she might wish, or be requested to, teach. Here are questions—in the context of a fictitious leader—to show the tone of the questioning:

◆ Allison, based on your background and current responsibilities, which of our programs do you find of interest or of most interest? If we worked with you to prepare, would you be willing to teach in one of these programs?

◆ John, now that you have experienced the Coaching for Impact Program, with the right preparation, are there any parts of this program that you might like to teach? Why do those parts of the program appeal to you?

◆ Bob, we have a goal to add two negotiation programs to our Business Skills College over the next nine months. They are Foundations of Negotiations and Advanced Negotiations. Given your background, could you see yourself teaching in either or both these programs?

◆ Linda, you are one of the people whose name always seems to come up when others in the company talk about leaders who manage their career well. Would you be willing to learn how to coteach in our Managing Your Career and Changing World programs? What might be the best ways to work with you to help you prepare to teach? What are some of the definite do's and don'ts in the way you like to learn?

◆ Dave, thank you for agreeing to teach as part of our faculty in our Leadership Development Program scheduled for this October. This is a program where we work individually with each executive to make sure he or she is comfortable with the teaching role. We would like you to teach in two or three of the nine modules. Of the list below, which seem to be the right fit or of greatest interest to you? What is the best way, from your perspective, to help you to be ready to teach in this program for the first time?

♦ Now that you have been through the entire program, I want to thank each one of the nine of you who have committed the next day and a half to the Selecting the Best Train-the-Trainer Program. Over the next six to 12 months, each of you will have the opportunity to observe and cotrain parts of the program one or more times. A goal is to reach the point that you and I agree that you are fully able and confident to cotrain the entire program with another experienced leader-teacher. As a starting point, which of the modules do you think will be easy, moderately difficult, or difficult for you to learn to teach? Please put each of the module titles in one of the three columns on the page in front of you. Then we will discuss your self-assessment of your readiness and capability and begin to design individual teaching progressions for each of you.

♦ ♦ ♦

Principle 2: Leaders Teach Best When They Are Confident That They Are Well Prepared to Teach Effectively

Gary Player was one of the top golfers in the world spanning several decades and is still remembered for his meticulous pregame preparation. His philosophy about preparation is simple and profound: "The more I practice, the luckier I get." John Wooden—educator, mentor, and the greatest college basketball coach of the 20th century—says: "Failing to prepare is preparing to fail." Steven Covey, the renowned leadership expert and best-selling author, states: "Begin with the end in mind." Fortune does shine favorably on those who plan and who are well prepared. Effective preparation breeds confidence, and confidence helps to bring out the best in everyone in just about all situations. Teaching and leader-teachers are no exception. If leaders are well prepared to teach, most leaders will truly look forward to teaching and will carry the day during their sessions.

The following preparation suggestions serve to strengthen the readiness and confidence of leader-teachers. First, build program-specific train-the-trainer certification programs. In many organizations, this approach also takes the form of an informal or formal certification process to teach a specific program. The topic of certification is complex and ranges from profession-specific certifying bodies (medicine, law, accounting, teaching) to company-specific in-house certification activities. For a leader-teacher program, the term is used to describe a leader-teacher who is qualified to teach or coteach a specific program. You may find some programs have very challenging teaching certification requirements such as Six Sigma or high-level project management and may include exams and supervised teaching to meet various levels of certification. That other programs have less challenging requirements and certification simply means that participants have completed a program-specific train-the-trainer process that qualifies the individual leader to teach. Here is a common sequence for the individual to join and become certified:

- *Expresses interest in the program.* Sometimes leaders express a willingness to serve as future leader-teachers of a particular program due to an inherent interest in the topic, concepts, and themes of the program. Some leaders may react to the "buzz" about a terrific program and say "Count me in." If the program is required for a specific employee group (for example, all managers), someone in this group may step up to share particular insight or out of a sense of duty to do their fair share of the teaching. Whatever the motivation, many leaders will sign up to teach without much prompting from you.
- *Participates in the program.* Participation alone often drives a willingness to serve as a leader-teacher. Sometimes leaders and other participant professionals serve as subject matter experts on a new program design team, and this spurs a desire to serve as a leader-teacher. Leaders who come to the program as a result of subject matter expert service or participation often have a keen sense of commitment to the program.
- *Participates in a program-specific train-the-trainer program and coteaches or team teaches a program.* This participation is the glue that retains and energizes leader-teachers. These train-the-trainer programs vary in length, from a half-day to several days, and may be taught by external consultants or by internal learning and development professionals. Note that if qualification to teach a class involves a licensed program from a consulting company, the consulting company will usually require that it provide the master trainer.

Learning and development professionals or other internal subject matter experts who serve as program champions often perform in the role of master trainers for specific internal train-the-trainer programs. The road map for these internal programs is a detailed instructor guide, manual, or facilitator's guide. This guide should be a treasure trove of detailed instructional tips and practices that master trainers follow to train others to teach the program.

Tips for Training the Trainer

Train-the-trainer programs provide leader-teachers with direct access to program content and the teaching flow and process elements of the program. The leaders also benefit from feedback and practice rounds of teaching. In addition, potential cotrainers are frequently identified when they become part of a leader-teacher community of practice.

A common limitation of program-specific train-the-trainer efforts is the relatively short amount of actual practice teaching time that each person receives. Teaching progressions (described under the third principle) help solve this issue.

Improving Leader-Teacher Skills

As noted, leaders and other professionals who participate in leader-teacher programs improve their ability to teach. However, teaching skills development is often shortchanged because these programs are heavily focused on content. Moreover, teaching comes more easily to some than to others. Great teaching is also a combination of nature, nurture, and purposeful preparation and practice. Though a certain amount of natural talent helps, hard work and dedication often make up for a deficit in these natural talents. In other words, teaching and facilitation skills can be learned. So if your organization is willing to invest in a high-potential leader-teacher, this can be a good investment for the organization and for you. Many external organizations offer classes and workshops that allow potential leader-teachers to learn and practice the craft of teaching, and the investment can pay benefits by producing highly effective teachers. Some organizations, such as BD, have developed these training programs in house.

Developing Training Skills

Developing Training Skills is a three-day course initially designed by Birgit Bergdoll and Noel Caffrey, two very talented learning and development professionals in Europe. The course has been offered in many parts of the world, and dozens of BD professionals and leaders have become better teachers and designers of active teaching and learning as a result. Facilitating Groups and Teams is multiday intense learning lab taught by Rod Napier, a pioneer in the field of group and team development. Graduates of this program develop a keen sense of design and facilitation skills within group, team, and organizational settings.

Similar programs are available in other companies and organizations and through vendor partners. Both these courses, similar to some program-specific train-the-trainer programs, make extensive use of feedback as a means of self-awareness and skill development. The outcome of these programs is that leaders are better prepared for their teaching roles while

---

Leader's Perspective

Birgit Bergdoll (BD's European human resources program manager) describes the role of train-the-trainer programs in this way: With the principle of leaders as teachers being seen as part of the leadership philosophy of the organization, many very enthusiastic people volunteer to take up this role in the company. Within this group, some have come forward with some or all the trainer skills, while others bring their enthusiasm and a need to develop these trainer skills further. This is where a thorough train-the-trainer concept needs to be developed. A train-the-trainer program can be in the form of teaching multipurpose training and facilitation skills, or it can be subject or content specific. Knowing about the topic you teach is one thing; being able to teach the facts and content—and develop personal insights that can be applied in a work setting by associates and leaders in a meaningful, active, and engaging way—is a different thing. The question is how to best involve the learner's heart and brain through various methods and activities to ensure that at the end of the program transfer to real work and life application will take place. This is where having a toolbox of active teaching methods helps both the experienced as well as the less experienced leader-teacher. These methods can be used in a wide array of teaching and learning situations.

gaining levels of confidence that are tremendously important for teaching and learning effectiveness.

Here are two other confidence-building paths:

♦ Senior leader preparation—customized, one-to-one helps. When senior executives prepare to be leader-teachers, learning and development professionals commonly help in the preparation through highly individualized one-to-one consulting (for example, see the sidebar case studies of Pat and Len). Make sure you use the time wisely and base your approach on the availability and learning style of each executive. Remember that if the high-level executive you prepared has a successful and enjoyable experience as a leader-teacher, then supporting your leader-teacher program is an easy decision.

♦ Select leader-teachers to introduce programs and serve as special speakers. Leaders require much less preparation in these roles compared with those who are individually teaching, coteaching, or team teaching the major parts of programs. Usually providing a few suggestions, guidelines, or questions will be enough preparation and ensure success. (See the sidebar for an example of these guidelines.)

♦ ♦ ♦

Guidelines for leader welcome and introduction—day 1 (10 to 15 minutes maximum):

♦ Welcome the participants.
♦ Briefly introduce the program by talking about the connection this program has to BD's Journey to Greatness.
♦ Briefly talk about BD's "Three Greats"—great performance, great contribution to society, and a great place to work—and how education and continuous self-development contribute to these.
♦ If you are a graduate of this program, discuss the benefits or outcomes that were provided to you as a result of taking the program.
♦ Discuss the importance of periodic self-assessment, use of feedback, possible use of assessment instruments, or other means

to continually improve one's performance and contribution to the company.

♦ Review the principles from the program. Choose one to which you particularly relate and very briefly discuss with the class why it is important to you.

Here are key principles for career development:

♦ Associate development is a shared responsibility, but each associate must take primary responsibility for his or her development.
♦ Career development is every leader's job.
♦ Development for continuous growth and improvement is encouraged and facilitated for all associates.
♦ The initial focus for development efforts is in an associate's current responsibilities.
♦ The primary vehicle for development at BD is work-related experiences.
♦ In-place, lateral (as well as vertical) moves are increasingly important for development.
♦ Performance management is a key part of an ongoing development process.
♦ Cross-geographic moves (especially international) require special consideration of an associate's fit and potential to excel in his or her position, complemented with sound development plans.
♦ Internal moves (lateral and vertical) are based on additional factors beyond performance in the associate's current assignment.

♦ ♦ ♦

Leader's Perspective

Wendy Witterschein, a key global leader with BD University who regularly prepares leaders to teach in key programs, says: Our leader-teachers don't wing it. They prepare for their faculty assignments with care and determination to be the best that they can be. For our flagship leadership programs, the preparation starts with a thorough briefing from me, and then study and reflection prior to the program. I recently taught with three senior leaders from our Europe Region, two who lead several countries, and one who leads a worldwide business platform. All were "rookies," but you would never know it by their teaching agility, their engagement, and their ability to orchestrate great discussions among the learners. This is a gift to the learners that we would not be able to replicate with professional or external faculty.

The use of these types of flexible guidelines regularly results in an upbeat and informative kickoff to the program. A similar approach can be used for guest speakers who will teach during the course or who might be invited as a lunchtime speaker. If you provide the guidelines to the guest speakers well in advance of the program, they will want to do well and will prepare themselves more than adequately for their visible teaching role. A light check-in with them is usually very helpful.

In preparing leaders to coteach and team teach, programs using the concept of two leader-teachers (that is, coteaching) or more than two leader-teachers (team teaching) have several advantages with very few downsides. Their advantages include

- No one leader-teacher feels that success of the program is dependent on him or her alone.
- There is backup if any business or personal emergency arises.
- There is a stronger chance that each leader will be able to teach in his or her comfort zone, from both content and instructional methodology perspectives, than if the leader taught solo.
- Coteaching and team teaching provide rich opportunities for learning content, leadership Teachable Points of View™, instructional methods, and facilitation skills from other leaders.
- They improve leader-teacher bench strength.
- They are a great way to stretch your comfort zone by taking on less familiar topics or modules and still know that you have one or more colleagues who can help if help is needed.
- They are a natural setting for peer coaching and exchanging constructive feedback with other leader-teachers.
- They create superb opportunities to network in your organization and to do talent scouting of other leaders.

Leveraging these advantages does not happen by accident. Certain agreements need to be in place for successful coteaching and team teaching, just as agreements and understandings need to be in play for teamwork between people in any setting. Several practices work very well. First, be clear about who is assigned or has offered to teach which specific learning modules or parts of modules:

- ◆ Make certain that each leader-teacher is satisfied and, hopefully, pleased with his or her assignments.
- ◆ Do not begin programs with any level of dissatisfaction in this regard.
- ◆ Confirm how the modules will be taught and facilitated.
- ◆ Be sure you can answer who is doing what alone and who is working on a section of the program together.
- ◆ Agree on how hand-offs between leader-teachers will be handled as primary teaching responsibilities shift throughout the program.

Another point for discussion by the teaching team is how and when to add supplementary comments when a coteacher or other member of the teaching team has center stage. A fine line exists between enriching the discussion and grabbing "air time." Discuss how and when it is best to exchange each other's observations, suggestions, perceptions, and feedback. Doing so allows you to take advantage of the peer coaching and feedback opportunities between the teaching team members. Get into the habit of discussing and reaching agreements on these points before the program starts and before and after each teaching or major session. Doing so frequently leads to trust and confidence between members of the teaching team, which in turn allows for easy midcourse adaptations and a sense of camaraderie. Each time teaching partners work together, there needs to be coteaching and team teaching collaboration.

◆ ◆ ◆

A Brief Profile of Pat, Senior Vice President and General Manager

Pat is a very successful senior vice president and general manager of one of your company's key global businesses. Pat is considered a high-potential leader for further executive responsibilities in the company. She and her colleague Len, the other senior vice president and general manager who will teach in the program, have been hand selected by the CEO and you to teach in the launch of this inaugural Leadership Development Program.

Pat's experience path started in sales, where she won several awards for the top territory sales professional in her region. In Pat's third and fourth years serving as a sales professional, she won the very distinguished President's Award as one of the top three sales professionals in the country. She was quickly promoted into the role of regional sales manager, where she excelled for more than three years. Subsequently, she headed the sales training function for two and a half years.

Pat then was promoted to the very visible role of marketing director for one of her company's hottest line of products, where she excelled for three years. This is her third year in her first senior vice president and general management role. Her undergraduate degree was in international business, and she graduated in the top 5 percent of her class. Her concentration was business strategy. Her MBA was completed at a top business school, where she and other students had to regularly present to their peer cohort and to their professors. Several courses used the case study method, and students learned quickly that they always needed to be on top of their game because the professors would call on any student at any time and expected spontaneous yet thoughtful responses.

Pat is a highly extroverted people person, and she projects confidence in just about all aspects of her role. For close to three years, she has regularly convened quarterly town meetings of hundreds of associates in her business around the world to communicate and teach about her business. She is also a regular guest speaker at various company gatherings in and outside her business. She enjoys meeting with different groups throughout the corporation.

Whenever Pat is not traveling for the business, she likes to get into the office early, usually by about 7:45 or 8:00 a.m. Her husband is able to get their children off to school in the morning four days out of the week. On the other day, Pat arrives at the office between 8:30 and 8:45 unless the CEO has called an earlier meeting, in which case their child care helper comes to the house early. Pat has an extremely busy schedule but can frequently be found in her office alone from 5:30 to 6:15 p.m. She generally tries to leave so that she can be home by 6:45 and spend time with her family and look over her children's homework. She has been a teacher at her church's Sunday school for about five years.

◆ ◆ ◆

◆ ◆ ◆

A Brief Profile of Len, Senior Vice President and General Manager

Len is also a senior vice president and general manager of one of the company's largest businesses. He is a PhD in chemical engineering by training. He originally made his name in the company as a result of his technical achievements and has long been thought of as one of the brightest executives in the company. He was a biochemistry major and physics minor at a prestigious small college. He earned an MBA from an Ivy League business school, where he concentrated in finance and organizational dynamics.

Len is very highly regarded by just about everyone in his global business and throughout the corporation. Similar to Pat, he is considered to have high potential for other executive roles. He is an analytical, creative, and amiable person with a fine sense of humor—except when he is under heavy stress, when he sometimes shifts into analytical problem-solving overdrive. He is introverted by nature and continuously works on developing excellent interpersonal skills.

Last year, Len attended an advanced executive education program at a top business school and was very intrigued by what he learned about himself during a day's work that was dedicated to the growing field of emotional intelligence. He has subsequently completed additional reading on the topic and has asked you for more resources on this subject. He has joked that his wife has told him that this is the most interesting and valuable topic he has studied since she has known him during his undergraduate days. A several-hour module of the three-day Leadership Development Program is dedicated to this topic.

Len does not readily seek opportunities to present to groups. But when he is in front of others, he does well. His well-earned credibility is clearly evident because of his deep company and product knowledge and because he has earned the respect of others through his highly effective day-to-day interactions with them. He actually has very little teaching experience in or out of work and is quick to say that he much prefers to work with small problem-solving groups than to be on center stage with larger groups. As part of Len's role as a general manager, he has to present to large groups at venues such as the national sales meetings and the end-of-year state-of-the-business meetings, where he presents in six locations across the globe. He has been quite open to, and has even requested, coaching in presentation skills when he has had to prepare for these presentations.

On a daily basis, Len is an early morning person and is at his best beginning at 7:15 a.m., when he is generally the first person in the office. He kids others by saying that when he retires in about a decade, he will have to train others on how to turn the lights on in the executive wing of the company headquarters. By 8:30, he is almost always immersed in the first of his meetings. Meetings of every shape and size generally consume much of his day when he is not traveling. When he is not traveling, he tries to complete his daily work by 5:15 to 5:30 p.m. so that he can arrive home before his wife and spend time with their children. He enjoys cooking, and he frequently gets dinner started as well.

In your role as head of the Leadership Academy, you and your Leadership Academy colleague now need to determine who will teach and coteach what topics in the program. Once this is determined, the two of you will be able to decide how to best help Pat and Len prepare for their teaching roles for the launch of the new Leadership Development Program.

◆ ◆ ◆

Principle 3: Leaders Should Teach at Their Own Level of Confidence and Effectiveness by Using Teaching Progressions

The guidelines presented here and the exercise at the end of this chapter offer real help when determining the readiness of leaders to teach in real business and organizational settings. You can use these suggestions and resources to determine what are the most appropriate teaching progressions for actual teaching situations. Progressions are used to enable leaders to assume increasingly challenging teaching assignments and build their teaching comfort level. From a goal-setting perspective, each progression should be "just out of reach but not out of sight."

Forms of Progressions

Progressions can be designed in many different ways to allow leaders to teach complex and challenging program content. Here are several suggestions to help leaders challenge and stretch their comfort zones:

- Observe others teaching next-level content.
- Assist an experienced leader-teacher teaching the new content.
- Encourage leader-teachers to present content based on actual experience or knowledge—the leader-teacher's "power alley."
- Teach challenging content for which you have had exposure for only a short period of time.
- Offer high-risk topics that require skillful facilitation or use engaging case studies to teach more difficult content.
- Be responsible for providing difficult feedback to class participants who are practicing new skills, solving difficult problems, or working on new or alternative strategies for business problems.
- Train others to teach a program.

Teaching progressions are essential elements of building and expanding a leaders-as-teachers process.

Determining What to Stretch

Determining what progressions fit with individual leader-teachers is both an art and a science. Here are five factors to keep in mind when deciding how to stretch your pool of leader-teachers.

First, each leader-teacher's background, content knowledge, and interests are different. Leaders have different backgrounds, interests, areas of experience, and possibly expertise. They may also have differences in their experience and confidence of subject matter content. Using the examples of Pat and Len (see the sidebars), Pat came from a sales and marketing background complemented by academic training in international business and strategy. Len was a PhD and chemical engineer by training. Each of these leaders will likely approach problems in a different way and will have preferences in what content areas he or she wishes to teach. Use these preferences and differences as assets and not problems by designing the right type of preparation and progressions for your leader-teachers.

Second, leaders have different experience teaching others and facilitating groups. Pat, as noted in the sidebar, likely has a deeply embedded life interest that includes teaching, coaching, and mentoring. She has important teaching experience that should be leveraged. Len is less experienced, and he is not naturally inclined to perform in front of others. Clearly, Pat's and Len's progressions will be different. Make sure you ask the right questions that will help them succeed. Here are some appropriate questions for determining the level of progression:

- ◆ "Would you be willing to present the modules on the 'good to great' principles and on developing your team's talent?"
- ◆ "Which modules would you be comfortable teaching by yourself, and which would you prefer to teach with me or someone else? I will be pleased to work with you to help you prepare and to ensure that you are confident in teaching these sections of the program."

Third, leaders learn and practice in different ways. Some leaders are comfortable with presenting a program and then reacting to positive and negative feedback. Other leaders are comfortable only if completely prepared and follow a strict teaching process. Still other leaders learn best by reading, seeing, or hearing a discussion on best practices. Here is a question that might be helpful in determining the learning and preparation style of the leader-teacher: "How do you learn best, and how would you like for me to work with you?"

Fourth, leaders learn at different paces and also have different teaching risk profiles. Some leaders are able to skip progressions that others are not. You will likely find leaders who are willing to risk teaching more challenging programs ("give it a shot") and others willing to teach only selected parts of a program. It is important to recognize these differences. However, just because someone says they can teach a particular topic does not make it true. Some leaders lack confidence and need to be gently nudged to take on more or to accelerate their progressions. Others may benefit from your words of caution.

In the case of Pat and Len, it is likely that Pat is experienced enough to teach certain programs more quickly than Len. On the other hand,

Len's analytical background will help him prepare to teach. A trusting relationship with each executive makes it easy for the executives to express what they would like to teach, how they would like to personalize their teaching approach, and how you can help them best prepare.

Fifth, leaders are very busy and generally have preferred times to meet and prepare to teach. In the case examples, working with Pat later in the day, beginning at about 5:30 p.m., is usually better than early in the day. Len, on the other hand, is a good candidate for an early morning meeting. What else might you want to factor in to the one-to-one preparation of both Pat and Len with regard to their teaching experience, subject matter expertise, personal interests, and general personality types? How might you use their experience, strengths, preferences, and differences when designing the right type of preparation and progressions for each of them? (See the appendix to this book for the content of the company's Leadership Development Program.)

◆ ◆ ◆

Determining Executive Teaching Experience

Determining executive teaching experience and readiness is a matter of targeted questioning. Use these questions to help you decide on the level of experience and readiness between two executives (tailor the questions to your own situation or program requirements):

◆ How are the backgrounds, roles, styles, and interests of the executives similar? How are they different?

◆ From what you know of the executives, how do you assess their respective readiness to teach in the Leadership Development Program?

◆ What factors are important to you in this setting to determine who should teach or coteach the various modules in the program?

◆ On an individualized basis, what approach would be most effective to take with each of the executives to ensure their preparation and readiness for their teaching roles?

◆ What work style factors for each of the executives should you consider in deciding how to best help these executives to prepare for their teaching roles?

◆ Keeping in mind that your plan and hope is that Pat and Len will teach in some of the future offerings of the Leadership

Development Program, are there any principles that you might employ regarding the use of teaching progressions with Pat and with Len in this launch of the program?

◆ ◆ ◆

Know Your Own Teaching Style

Not only do leader-teachers require training and coaching, successful leader-teachers must also take time to consider their own teaching style to really operate at the top of their game. Most people will naturally gravitate to what has worked best for them in other situations when they have had to learn or relearn information or when they needed to facilitate a session in a group or team setting. Some leaders want to read the instructor's manual several times. Some will mark it up with highlighters. Others want to do extensive background reading on the subject. Yet others will want to do a quick run through alone or with others. Some leaders will want a last-minute word of encouragement before teaching, while others are best left alone. As a learning professional, you should encourage leader-teachers to find the approach that works best for them.

The Importance of Feedback

Entire books, chapters, and articles have been written about the how-tos and value of feedback in professional and personal settings. For the purpose of developing, preparing, and improving the teaching performance of leaders, these two guidelines have served my teams well over many years:

1. Ensure that rich, credible, and well-timed feedback is integrated into any train-the-trainer program and leader-teacher preparation process you implement in your organization.
2. All leaders, including senior executives, are able to continuously improve their teaching as a result of well-delivered, well-timed, and courageous feedback throughout the teaching and learning process.

Used correctly, feedback reinforces desirable teaching performance and helps leaders to understand areas for improvement in their teaching. Effective feedback can also help identify alternative methods to teach or facilitate difficult topics. It is essential to build the expectation that the process of sharing feedback is a form of healthy peer support and is an important continuous improvement element of the leaders-as-teachers process. Do what is necessary to make feedback a way of doing business and a responsibility of being a leader-teacher in your organization.

It is also important that your individualized work with senior leaders and key executives model effective feedback. Executives typically have very few people in their lives willing to provide them with straight talk and feedback. This is frequently true in many aspects of their roles. By working with leader-teachers at all levels in the organization from their early preparation through their actual teaching and facilitation roles, you have a unique opportunity to help leaders continuously improve their performance in this very visible aspect of their responsibilities. By helping leader-teachers to be successful—yes, even to be stars when they teach—you create the conditions for a positive self-fulfilling prophecy to form about the leaders-as-teachers process and of your leadership and involvement. When executed with high levels of professionalism, your contributions will be valued and respected.

It is also very important for feedback between coteachers and team teachers to be shared. Again, if you establish this practice from the beginning as a way of doing business, it becomes a natural occurrence and a positive element in your organization's culture. Feedback usually serves to strengthen collegial relationships and also improves the teaching and learning process.

Feedback Models

What is the best way to provide feedback once the expectation has been set that feedback is part of the leaders-as-teachers process in your organization? Two models of effective feedback have long track records and can be implemented in almost all organizations.

One model is sometimes referred to as the "sandwich model of feedback." This approach has three steps. It should be preceded with a brief discussion and agreement between the leader-teacher and feedback provider(s) about how the steps will be used to help strengthen the quality and impact of the teaching session by the leader. The feedback providers typically are fellow leader-teachers or learning and development professionals. The three steps are:

1. The feedback providers state what they perceived went well that helped participants learn.
2. Then the feedback providers state what they perceived did not go well or that could have been more effective or taught differently.
3. The feedback providers and the leader-teacher discuss and confirm what positive action will or could be taken the next time he or she has an opportunity to teach.

This approach is referred to as the sandwich method of feedback because the second step of constructive feedback is surrounded with positive observations and positive agreements going forward in steps 1 and 3. This method of feedback can be very helpful and, with variations, has been used in many settings for many years. It is one of the simplest of all feedback models.

A second method of feedback involves a combination of self-assessment and feedback from one or more observers, who, similar to the sandwich method, are typically fellow leader-teachers or learning and development professionals. This approach has four primary steps, with substeps. Similar to the sandwich method, there should be a discussion and agreement between the leader-teacher and feedback providers about how the steps will be used to help strengthen the quality and impact of the teaching-learning process.

Step 1 is that the leader-teacher and feedback providers discuss what will be taught and how it will be taught. This develops a common understanding and also anticipation of what to look for and expect.

Step 2: Following the teaching session, the leader-teacher discusses his or her self-assessment with the feedback providers. The first part of the self-assessment focuses entirely on the positive aspects of the teaching as viewed by the leader-teacher. The second element of the self-assessment described by the leader-teacher responds to the question, "What, if anything, would I have changed if I had a chance to teach this session over?" In the final element of the self-assessment, the leader-teacher describes how he or she would teach the session in the future.

Step 3: Following the self-assessment by the leader-teacher, the feedback providers essentially employ the sandwich feedback steps described above. Their context includes both their observation and perception of the teaching session and the self-assessment that has just been described by the leader-teacher who taught the session:

- The feedback providers state what they perceived went well that helped participants learn.
- Then the feedback providers state what they perceived did not go well or that could have been more effective or taught differently.
- The feedback providers and the leader-teacher discuss and confirm what positive action will or could be taken the next time he or she has an opportunity to teach.

Step 4 in this feedback cycle consists simply of the leader-teacher and feedback providers informally discussing and further debriefing the teaching session, the self-assessment, and feedback. The goal of this short discussion is personal learning and awareness.

The integration of feedback mechanisms in the leaders-as-teachers process is designed to have a positive impact on learning by focusing on the continuous improvement of leader-teachers. Set the ground rules and ensure that the leader-teachers are on board with the goal of continuously improving as teachers and facilitators. It is then possible to effectively use feedback "here, there, everywhere" as part of the leaders-as-teachers process. It should be a normal aspect of your organization's leaders-as-teachers process.

Principle 4: Use Active Teaching and Training Methods in Program Design

Mel Silberman—the author of *101 Ways to Make Training Active* and numerous other books on active and effective training and learning—describes active training this way:

> Yes, there is a whole lot more to training than telling! Learning is not an automatic consequence of pouring information into another person's head. It requires the learner's own mental and physical involvement. Lecturing and demonstrating, by

themselves, will never lead to real, lasting learning. Only training that is active will.

What makes training "active"? When training is active, the participants do most of the work. They use their brains—studying ideas, solving problems, and applying what they learn. Active training is fast-paced, fun, supportive, and personally engaging. Often, participants are out of their seats, moving about and thinking aloud.

Why is it necessary to make training active? In order to learn something well, it helps to hear it, see it, ask questions about it, and discuss it with others. Above all else, we need to "do it." That includes figuring out things by ourselves, coming up with examples, rehearsing skills, and doing tasks that depend on the knowledge we have. (Silberman 2005, 1)

The next chapter explores the active teaching and learning process, including specific active teaching and learning methods that leader-teachers can use both in and outside the classroom. Designating active teaching as the fourth principle is meant to demonstrate the importance of the practice to the overall success of a leader-teacher program. Program participants learn best when all their senses are involved and classroom activities are connected to their work and life experiences. PowerPoint slides do have their place in the classroom, but there are many other more effective teaching methods.

Chapter 7 offers a carefully selected variety of highly effective active teaching methods and tools that help the learning process come alive. Examples of active teaching and learning methods range from case studies to problem-solving groups to action learning and innovation teams to discussion groups to learning partners and peer teaching and coaching rounds. The memory "half-life" of this type of learning experience is much greater than that of primarily one-way, static teaching and learning methods. Once leaders are introduced to these active teaching methods, their teaching comfort level grows and they become more effective teachers. Most important, this new comfort level and sense of success and connection with the participants makes your job of recruiting and training new leader-teachers much easier.

◆ ◆ ◆

Implementation Activity 1: The Four Principles of Leader-Teacher Recruitment and Preparation Exercise

This activity is designed as both an assessment and planning tool to determine if the four principles of leader-teacher recruitment and preparation: (1) are currently operational in your organization, and (2) can be established or strengthened in your organization.

Place a check next to Yes or No in the second column. Describe your plans to establish or strengthen each of the four principles of leader-teacher preparation in the third column:

Principle	Are these principles currently operational?	Plans to establish or strengthen each of the four principles:
1. Recruiting and matching leaders' background, expertise, responsibilities, and teaching interests within program content and teaching assignments increases leaders' readiness to teach.	Yes _____ No _____	
2. Leaders teach best when they are confident that they are well prepared to teach—do you have mechanisms to build leader-teacher confidence?	Yes _____ No _____	
3. Teaching readiness and individualized progressions are essential to building leader-teacher confidence and effectiveness. Do you have mechanisms to build leader-teacher readiness?	Yes _____ No _____	
4. The preparation and effectiveness of leader-teachers are made easier when active teaching and training methods are used in program design. Do you use active training methods?	Yes _____ No _____	

Implementation Activity 2: Do the Conditions Exist for Leaders to Volunteer to Teach in Your Organization?

This activity allows you to (1) assess whether the seven key conditions exist in your organization that encourage leaders to volunteer to teach, and (2) plan to establish or strengthen each of the seven conditions.

Place a check next to Yes or No in the second column. Describe your plans to establish or strengthen each of the seven conditions to volunteer to teach in your organization.

Condition	Does this condition currently exist?	Plan to establish or strengthen this condition:
1. Encouraged and recognized to teach by the organization's culture.	Yes _____ No _____	
2. Able to share what they know including their leadership Teachable Points of View™.	Yes _____ No _____	
3. Add business value and contribute to building individual and organizational capability.	Yes _____ No _____	
4. Supported by learning and development professionals in the preparation period in advance of actually teaching.	Yes _____ No _____	
5. Confident they will be successful when they teach.	Yes _____ No _____	
6. Able to enjoy themselves and take pride in their contribution, in part, because their teaching assignments will be matched with their interests, backgrounds, experience, and capabilities.	Yes _____ No _____	
7. Control their busy calendars and are comfortable with the total amount of time necessary to prepare and to teach.	Yes _____ No _____	

Make Learning Content Come Alive

Helping Leaders Spark Active Learning Experiences

It is not what you tell your participants that counts. What counts is what they take away with them. That's because the more you tell them, the more they will forget. Moreover, you can't learn for them. They must do it themselves. Your role as a trainer therefore is to spark and guide their learning and help to make it last.
—Mel Silberman, *101 Ways to Make Training Active*

◆ ◆ ◆

What's Inside This Chapter?

Structuring content to ensure both the participant and the teacher are actively engaged in the learning process is an important component in building a successful leader-teacher program. This chapter demonstrates the use of active teaching approaches to learning and offers a baker's dozen of active teaching methods for use by leader-teachers. These multipurpose teaching and facilitation methods can be adapted and used for many content areas. Most important, these methods are easily adaptable for use in cultures around the world. The methods include

- storytelling
- Teachable Points of View™
- skillful questioning

- small group work and discussions
- problem solving
- case studies, exercises, and simulations
- peer teaching and coaching
- town meetings
- media and technology blending
- mini-lectures
- "parking lot" issues
- learning journals
- learning gems through learning debriefs.

The second section of this chapter offers a three-level framework for designing and organizing most program content. The active learning framework relies on program participants being actively involved in their own learning, thus increasing learning retention through personalization of the learning process. Most important, the design model enables natural follow-through and application by the learner. From the leader's point of view, content designed this way makes the job of teaching easier and more enjoyable. The chapter ends with two exercises to help you apply these concepts.

◆ ◆ ◆

Death by PowerPoint

All of us have endured classes worthy of the familiar catchphrase "death by PowerPoint"—drowning recitations of content based on bulleted lecture notes without any attempt to engage participants or facilitate the learning. If this experience was a movie, it would be called *The Class That Stood Still.* Clearly, this method of lecture is ineffective, but unfortunately it is still widely used in many live classroom settings.

Active Teaching

Active teaching is just the opposite of death by PowerPoint. Active teaching ignites learning and engages participants. Active teaching also

- Captures participants' attention and energy and maintains it throughout the learning experience

- Creates enthusiasm and the motivation to learn and teach
- Involves participants' different types of intelligence and processing modes: cognitive (thinking), behavioral (acting), and affective (feelings, attitudes, and values)
- Stretches learners' thinking comfort zones
- Provides "chemistry" for enthusiastic and meaningful discussions
- Encourages intellectual questioning
- Expands learners' comfort zones
- Involves learning by doing, experiencing, risk taking, and experimenting
- Encourages individualized thinking and problem solving
- Encourages social interaction, cooperative learning, and problem solving
- Helps participants to teach and coach each other
- Occurs in a variety of places, including classrooms, field and action learning projects, and internships, and through certain types of technology-enabled learning
- Paves the way for the use of technology to expand learning capabilities as well as information and knowledge sharing

---

Leader's Perspective

Bill Kozy (executive vice president, BD) says: BD University has quickly evolved into the primary learning opportunity in our company. It brings a unique approach that can effectively educate the BD associate on the company's key leadership and management expectations—dealing directly with the behaviors and the performance factors that create successful careers. At the same time, each participant is immersed in a learning space that also focuses on his or her individual strengths and opportunities for personal improvement. If you actively participate, and BD University is participative learning, you will leave the session with a clear idea of what it takes at BD to do well and a full set of ideas on how you can get there. Our associates now recognize this, and, as a leader-teacher, this creates a high-energy engagement process and a very positive way to partner in the personal development of others.

- Crystallizes valuable experiences into unforgettable "learning gems" with high levels of learning retention
- Prepares learners to implement and take action on their learning
- Increases the likelihood that the learning experience will have an observable, measurable impact as a result of the factors listed above.

In short, programs designed with active training methods produce memorable teaching and learning results. Learners and leaders come back for more.

Active Adult Learning Is No Secret

Great teachers have known for centuries that it is important to actively involve individuals in their own learning. Confucius is known for using active learning and teaching methods. The Greek philosopher Socrates used questions to stimulate deep thinking and contemplation. In the 20th century, John Dewey, an iconic philosopher and educator, challenged dogmatic, teacher-centered educational approaches and stressed the importance of "learning by doing." Louis Raths, a student of Dewey, further developed learning and facilitation theories that stressed the importance of personalizing the teaching and learning process. For the past four to five decades, great educators and master facilitators such as Sidney Simon, Merrill Harmin, Howard Kirschenbaum, Rod Napier, and Leland Howe have created tremendously valuable models for personalizing education and tapping into the power and wisdom of groups.

Very useful research has evolved and has focused on how and under what conditions learning occurs. Several highlights of this modern period include the University of Minnesota's Roger and David Johnson, who focused on cooperative learning, and Malcolm Knowles, who focused on adult educational theory and practice. Contemporary educators such as Allison Rossett and Elliott Masie are well-known proponents of blended learning methods, including the use of technology, to actively engage students in learning. Other contemporary standard-bearers for active learning are Mel Silberman and Bob Pike. Both these educators have trained thousands of trainers and educators in techniques of learner-centered teaching and active teaching methods and influenced a whole generation in the practice.

Methods for Active Teaching, Training, and Learning

The Chinese philosopher Confucius offered this active learning endorsement many centuries ago:

> When I hear, I forget.
> What I see, I remember.
> What I do, I understand.

The contemporary learning guru Mel Silberman (1998, 3) suggested the following restatement of Confucius's famous quotation:

> When I hear, I forget.
> When I hear and see, I remember a little.
> When I hear, see, and ask questions or discuss with someone else, I begin to understand.
> When I hear, see, discuss, and do, I acquire knowledge and skill.
> When I teach to another, I master.

Silberman succinctly describes the rationale behind using active teaching and learning methodology. Teaching *is* an important catalyst for the on-going development of leaders, and the value is evident on the face of every leader at the end of every successful class. This sense of satisfaction is also what brings leader-teachers back to teach again and again.

A Baker's Dozen of Terrific Active Teaching Methods

Here are 13 active teaching methods—a baker's dozen—that constitute solid, tested ways to actively engage participants in their learning. Silberman and others also describe many other active teaching methods in their writings. You can tailor these methods to specific program content and the needs of participants, and your leader-teacher will be a star in the classroom—and even online.

Storytelling

The first active teaching method is storytelling. For thousands of years, cultures have used storytelling not only as a form of entertainment but also as a way to preserve and hand down traditions and communicate societal expectations to future generations. The power of storytelling is not lost on modern scholars. A *Harvard Business Review* article titled "The Four Truths of the Story Teller" (Guber 2007) identified the four truths of the effective use of storytelling in organizations:

- Truth to the teller: This is the congruency and authenticity test between word and deed, between walking and talking, on the part of the leader who tells the story. Essentially, is the storyteller credible?
- Truth to the audience: Is the message communicated in a way and with the correct meaning so that it has the desired impact and is credible?
- Truth to the moment: Can the storyteller read his or her audience and adapt the delivery so that it has the desired effect?
- Truth to the mission: Can the storyteller communicate in a way so that it is clear that the cause is of such importance that the cause itself exceeds that of self?

An earlier *Harvard Business Review* article, "Telling Tales" (Denning 2004) stressed the importance of going beyond analysis and using storytelling to reach into the hearts of people to truly motivate them. This article describes seven uses of effective storytelling and the importance of changing the narrative pattern for each use to achieve management goals. The seven uses are

- sparking action
- communicating who you are
- transmitting values
- fostering collaboration
- taming the grapevine
- sharing knowledge
- leading people into the future.

Douglas Reddy (2002), in his evidence-based article "How Storytelling Builds Next-Generation Leaders," describes five elements of effective stories:

- Context specific, in alignment with a company's business strategies and goals.
- Level-appropriate: The context should be specific to the types of roles and responsibilities of the participants.
- Told by respected role models; this point tracks directly with Guber's notion of the four truths of storytellers.
- Has drama—the story has compelling points that capture the head, heart, and attention of the learner.
- Has high learning value—has a behavior-altering learning impact and value.

How can leader-teachers use stories? Clearly, storytelling is valuable as a teaching method. So here are a few hints for using storytelling as an action teaching and learning method:

- Use a well-told story to make a point, possibly a leadership Teachable Point of View™. Then let participants react to the story individually or in groups. Encourage participants to extract very important points—learning gems—from your story or those of participants or other faculty.
- Have students tell stories to each other or aloud in class for all to hear. These stories might have obvious business or leadership points to make. The stories could also serve as analogies or metaphors, with the most important points coming out in the debriefing session that should follow the story. Make sure to debrief the story: What is its importance? What are its key points? What are its implications and opportunities for application?
- Use stories told by participants or faculty at any point in the program—at the beginning; in the middle; or as a way to summarize a lesson, module, or program.
- There are a number of good books and instructional programs on storytelling that can help you and program participants hone your skills. Use these books and seminars as professional development resources.

Teachable Points of View™

The second active teaching method is Teachable Points of View™. The late sports commentator Howard Cosell coined the term "up close and personal" as way of introducing a person who he was going to interview. Up close and personal is an excellent way to think about this concept (see chapter 2 for more on Teachable Points of View™ and its roots in Noel Tichy's work). The following three points are the working assumptions for using this active teaching and learning tool:

1. As a leader and role model, develop your own personal Teachable Points of View™ and expect those whom you are teaching to develop their own.
2. Leaders are always more effective than they otherwise would be if they have points of view on a range of issues, such as what it really takes for business success, ethics, and confidentiality; execution; individual and team effectiveness; and developing others.
3. There always needs to be consistency between leaders' words and actions. Anything less is typically viewed as inconsistent at best and as hypocritical, unethical, or laughable at worst.

Here are seven suggestions on how to include leadership Teachable Points of View™ as a versatile method in your active teaching and learning tool box. First, communicate your points of view in vivid stories, anecdotes, or reflections of your career. To do so, use some of the suggestions described above under the first method, storytelling.

Second, have participants prepare concise written statements summarizing a leadership Teachable Point of View™ they hold on a topic that is important to them.

Third, provide opportunities for participants to state their leadership Teachable Points of View™ either directly from their written statement or in story form. Make sure to have the participants also describe how they actually act on these strongly held beliefs, reinforcing the importance of consistency between words and actions.

Fourth, use points of view to introduce or anchor sessions that leader-teachers or participants present and facilitate. One way to do this is have one or two participants open up each session of a several-day program by sharing one of their points of view. This can be arranged by having the participants post their name and the title or theme of their point of view on flip chart paper that is posted in a convenient location in the room. This reinforces the expectation that the participants will share their point of view with others. You could work your way down the list in the order of the sign-ups. However, once you see the titles or themes that are posted, you could select the ones that match particular lessons or modules.

Fifth, refer back to specific leadership Teachable Points of View™ throughout the program once they have been presented and shared in class. This is an excellent way to connect program content with the personal perspectives of both the faculty and participants.

Sixth, in addition to embracing the various perspectives and leadership Teachable Points of View™ expressed by participants, they could also be used to stimulate dialogue and even debate on a topic that might have some controversy or different perspectives, such as handling different challenging business growth and performance situations; handling ethical and nonethical dilemmas; choosing the correct strategy; operating at your best under pressure; managing family, community, and work responsibilities; and managing dual career marriages or relationships.

Seventh, the selection and use of quotations by participants can often serve as an easy way to help express their leadership points of view. Over about a five-year period, this technique has been used by one organization as part of its leadership programs. As part of their prework, participants are asked to bring one or more quotations that represent their own point of view on a leadership topic of their choice. These quotations are also posted on flip chart paper and shared at various points during the program. Several hundred of these quotations have now been collected and housed on the program's intranet website for future use by graduates of the program in their actual work settings and in presentations they may make.

Skillful Questioning

The third active teaching method is skillful questioning. Great questions swing the door open for great thinking, communications, and learning. Bad questions have the opposite effect. The use of effective questioning techniques is a hallmark of effective active teaching and is both a skill and an art form. The ability to ask effective questions takes practice. Here are some suggestions on using questions to stimulate active learning:

- Use one or more thought-provoking questions to introduce a session.
- Let participants answer aloud in the large group, discuss in small groups, or do a combination of both.
- To stimulate broad and creative thinking, use open-ended questions.
- Closed-ended questions can be very effectively used to make decisions and to narrow and deepen broad discussions and thinking.
- Use clarifying questions to confirm understanding and to "defuzz" fuzzy concepts and notions.
- Use short questions with clear language to avoid confusion about what you are asking.
- Do not ask too many questions at one time. There is a fine line between feeling stimulated to learn and feeling interrogated.
- Be clear about your learning goals. Let these goals determine what questions you will ask.
- Follow up effective questions with great listening. Really hear what is being said and avoid rushing into a next question or response.
- Use questions for effective learning interviews. These could be interviews on a topic or range of topics that you conduct of one participant with others observing and learning. It could be an interview that you conduct with several participants, or that participants do with you as others observe. You could have participants interview each other. Consider following up interviews of all types with learning debriefs to help surface key points that have been learned.

♦ There are many times when you can make a statement or formulate a question that will trigger valuable thinking. Consider using questions first before making a statement or offering your perspective.

If you are interested in knowing more about questions, there are two excellent resources. The first is *The 7 Powers of Questions,* by Dorothy Leeds (2000), which describes seven benefits and outcomes of questions and provides many examples of effective questioning techniques:

♦ Questions demand answers.

♦ Questions stimulate thinking.

♦ Questions give us valuable information.

♦ Questions put you in control.

♦ Questions get people to open up.

♦ Questions lead to high-quality listening.

♦ Questions get people to persuade themselves.

The second excellent resource is *Leading with Questions: How Leaders Find the Right Solutions by Knowing What to Ask* by Michael Marquardt (2005). This is an especially helpful book for actual skill development, including how to determine what questions or what type of questions to use across a variety of business and work situations. Pay particular attention to the chapter titled "The Art of Asking Questions."

Small Group Work and Discussions
The fourth active teaching method is small group work and discussions. The topic of small group facilitation and the use of group and cooperative learning design are fundamental elements of experiential and active teaching and learning.

Here are four suggestions on how you can use these techniques. First, if you are not used to working with small groups and facilitating discussions, start slowly with very simple designs.

Second, small groups could range from learning pairs to groups of threes, fours, fives, sixes, or even larger. The simplest of all small group designs is to put participants in a small group configuration and then assign them a task topic or discussion topic to work on for a designated period of time. Groups then report their findings, conclusions, or perspectives on the topic.

Third, small groups are generally ideal for a wide variety of cooperative learning experiences where peers and colleagues gain from the experiences of others.

Fourth, experiment with group designs. For example, combine groups. For a first discussion or problem-solving task, work in groups of twos or threes. For the second step, combine the groups into fours or sixes, and then have them report the results of their discussions or problem solving back to the large group.

Problem Solving

The fifth active teaching method is problem solving. Business problems are excellent fodder for active teaching and learning. Here are some examples you might use in your program design:

- ◆ Real-time business problems, such as leadership and ethical dilemmas.
- ◆ Larger-scale action learning projects—typically, business challenges or problems facing an organization or part of an organization that require a team to work on for a designated period of time, which could be weeks or even months. Typically, the team's recommendations are reported back to senior managers.
- ◆ Prewritten dilemmas or business problems—usually written by subject matter experts, often with the assistance of instructional designers or learning professionals. They fall into the category of "What would you do if...?" or "How would you handle this situation?" or "A problem facing this team or business unit is..." type situations. This type of learning activity might require a combination of individualized work combined with small group or team discussions and problem solving.

Facilitating Case Studies, Predesigned Exercises, and Simulations

The sixth active teaching method is facilitating case studies, predesigned exercises, and simulations. Harvard Business School pioneered the use of the business case study method. Many variations exist on the basic common practice formula, but the most common theme revolves around the "What would you do in this situation?" Predesigned exercises and simulations differ from case studies in structure and design, but all deal with the challenges that leaders, managers, and professionals face in their work. Both methods require high participant involvement and a moderate to high level of teaching and facilitation skills.

Peer Teaching and Peer Coaching

The seventh active teaching method is peer teaching and peer coaching. The amount of collective experience and education in a typical management or leadership development program is always impressive. In a group of 30 participants, you might rack up 450 years of work experience and dozens of advanced academic degrees. In addition, each participant and leader-teacher has access to many hundreds of other people—not to mention access to limitless websites, blogs, and other technological and nontechnological resources, including social networks. Peer teaching and peer coaching tap into this rich pool of experience and resources. There are many types of teaching designs utilizing peers in teaching or coaching roles that leaders can facilitate.

Let's look at three examples of how to use these resources. First, a video on "group think" and effective decision making is shown. The leader-teacher then facilitates a large group discussion focused on several debriefing questions related to the video. The leader-teacher presents a 15-minute mini-lecture and outlines a decision-making model that is uniformly used in that company. The class is then divided into peer teaching groups of four participants. Within the groups, participants are asked to teach each other ways that they can use the decision-making model in their daily work while avoiding the pitfalls of group think. The best of these peer-generated ideas are then shared in the large group. The leaders who are teaching the program comment and augment the peer-coaching ideas, as appropriate.

Second, in preparation for a module on emotional intelligence, pre-reading and a self-assessment instrument is assigned as prework. The module begins by dividing the class into five groups who are assigned to work at each of five flip chart easels. Their task is to teach each other everything they know and have learned from their preprogram assignments. After 15 minutes of flip charting their ideas, the leader-teacher then facilitates sharing across the room. Some of the best ideas from the peer-teaching small group work are shared aloud with the larger group. The leader-teacher further supplements the peer teaching by adding his or her comments and knowledge of the subject.

Third, as part of a module on execution, the class is divided into peer-coaching groups of threes. Once the participants are with their peer-coaching trios, the class is taught a simple method for peer coaching. The process or cycle of peer coaching consists of three rounds. In each round, one person is the focus person and the two others serve as peer coaches. The topic of this peer-coaching session is overcoming an execution challenge that the participant faces in his or her real work. After the three rounds are completed, a learning debrief is facilitated by the leader-teacher.

Conducting Informative Town Meetings

The eighth active teaching method is conducting informative town meetings. By their very nature, town meetings are interactive. Usually, one or several organizational leaders preside and serve a dual communications and teaching role. Usually the leader or leaders make opening comments and then field questions.

Let's look at three ideas for building town meetings into active experiences in learning programs. First, invite a respected executive in your company to conduct a town meeting as part of a management, leadership, sales, or business skill program. It is best to have the town meeting after at least a third or half of the program has been completed. Have participants prepare at least one question per person in advance. Also, agree in advance who will ask the first question to get the ball rolling, and then let the meeting fly!

Second, after the town meeting, conduct a learning debriefing session. The first thing to do is to ask the participants to reflect individually on what they heard and if there are points that link to the concepts of the program. Then spend 10 to 15 minutes in small group discussions, followed by a large group discussion of what was communicated and what was learned in the town meeting.

Third, extract the major points from the learning debrief. Ask participants to find connections to the content of the program. These could be points of agreement, points of disagreement, or points that can be explored further in or outside the program.

Blending Media and Technology with Skillful Teaching and Facilitation

The ninth active teaching method entails blending media and technology with skillful teaching and facilitation. Limitless possibilities exist to tap into the power of technology. Whether the access is through the use of blogs, Internet sites, social networking tools, YouTube, Second Life (see chapter 3), or media prepared specifically for learning and training purposes, the choices are exciting and perhaps a bit challenging. For the learning professional, the great variety of technology-driven learning solutions offers both active and passive learning pathways. Here are some ways to follow an active path to learning, teaching, and facilitation via the use of technology:

- Use interactive Webinars to reach across geographies and time zones. Really encourage participation through voice access as well as through questions and comments submitted synchronously online.
- As opportunities present themselves, follow up individually or in small groups for learning and work-related reinforcement purposes after the Webinars.
- Combine podcasts, Webinars, and assigned asynchronous material with live classroom learning. Any of these technologies can

be used as prework, in-program supplemental material, or for follow-up and reinforcement purposes.

♦ Teach synchronous coursework online. Then have scheduled individual and group follow-up sessions that could be done by phone, by video, or in person.

♦ Periodic classroom sessions could be used to supplement e-learning courseware.

♦ Use videoconferencing to conduct short, live learning sessions.

♦ Use social networking technologies to share information, conduct threaded discussions, solve problems, and teach short lessons.

♦ Assign material that needs to be searched on the web and then blend it into a live classroom session.

♦ Use electronic simulations during classroom discussions as a way of teaching a wide range of business, management, and leadership topics.

♦ Introduce an e-learning course with a live classroom session. End this learning cycle with a live classroom session or sessions to help integrate and synthesize the learning.

Use Mini-Lectures

The 10th active teaching method is to use mini-lectures. Though the term "lecture" might seem out of place in a list of active learning methodologies, short lectures can be effective and engage the learner. As you might guess, how you approach this methodology makes all the difference. Here are some suggestions for using mini-lectures:

♦ Try to limit uninterrupted, one-way communication to 15 or 20 minutes.

♦ Introduce a mini-lecture with an attention-getting activity, sometimes called a "grabber." Grabbers could include polling the group or asking questions, a quick story, an anecdote, a funny graphic, or a comic strip snapshot. You could also use a very short pretest that tracks to the mini-lecture content. At the end of the mini-lecture, verbally review the answers to the pretest to clarify information points and to reinforce learning.

- If you are going to use PowerPoint slides, limit the number to 10 or fewer. These should be visual supplements and not speaking scripts.
- Consider starting your mini-lecture with your summary. Then end it with the same or a variation of the same summary. The old adage "Say what you are going to say, say it, and say what you have said" is still wise counsel.
- Always surround the mini-lecture with active learning material and activity.
- Break up the one-way communication by stopping one or two times and asking if there is a volunteer to summarize what you have said and what he or she has heard up to that point, in that volunteer's own words.
- Reserve time at the end of the mini-lecture for questions.
- For longer blocks of time, consider doing a series of two or three mini-lectures interspersed with activities, questions that you pose, or questions from the participants.

Tackling "Parking Lot" Issues

The 11th active teaching method is to tackle "parking lot" issues, which are meeting topics that are put off for discussion at a later date. Generally, a topic becomes a parking lot issue when it seems tangential to the purpose of the meeting or the group had insufficient time or resources to deal with it. In the context of active teaching methods, parking lot topics are often custom made for teachable moments.

Consider these eight hints on taking advantage of these topics. First, introduce the parking lot concept during the introduction of the program. Hang flip chart paper for just this purpose, and mark it "Parking Lot."

Second, during the program's introduction, set the ground rules. It is OK for either the participants or faculty to post a parking lot item. State how often or when the parking lot issues and topics will be addressed. Clarify if anything is out of bounds and will not be handled in this program.

Third, parking lot issues are generally responded to by the leaders who teach the program.

Fourth, it is best to address parking lot issues each day during a multiday program. Sometimes this may not be possible, so be sure to designate times when the issues will be addressed. Try not to let two days to go by in a multiday program without addressing at least some items in the parking lot. For a one-day program, make certain that any parking lot issues are resolved by the end of the day if not earlier in the session.

Fifth, make sure that all parking lot topics have been discussed by the conclusion of the program. Not to do so raises questions of credibility for the leader-teachers.

Sixth, before addressing each item, clarify and confirm your understanding of the topic or issue, and most important, what might be a less obvious issue below the surface.

Seventh, certain items need to be addressed by specialists in the company. Some of these fall into the human resources bucket, so it is good to have an experienced and respected human resources professional on call.

Eighth, sometimes a program—especially a management or leadership development program—serves as the lightning rod for surfacing the "unspeakable." This is frequently the "elephant in the room" that nobody has wanted to touch, but somehow the program has provided a safe haven for someone to finally say what others have been thinking. Deal with these issues directly. These are valuable and necessary discussions. Sometimes the issue's size, scope, or importance to the company is beyond what the faculty can or should tackle. I have had this occur every once in awhile and even have arranged for the company CEO to come to the program on the following day. In that example, the CEO's involvement and concern was an enormously valuable experience. The dialogue with the class also convinced the CEO to take action on something that was on his to-do list but that he moved way up in time and priority after visiting the program to hear the issues. The CEO's credibility continued to grow in the weeks after the program as courageous actions were taken and changes made in company policy and practice.

Reflection through Learning Journals

The 12th active teaching method is reflection through learning journals. Learning journals are used for much more than note taking, although they do serve that important function. Learning journals are also where program participants record their personal insights and reflections as well as integrate and synthesize their learning experiences. Without well-maintained and up-to-date journals, it is very hard to pull together the many learning experiences as the course progresses and as it comes to an end. Learning journals require timely and regular entries throughout the course of a program.

When are journals appropriate? What makes this information important to understand for leader-teachers and learning leaders? There are certain types of programs where all learners, or at least almost all, will benefit tremendously from keeping a learning journal. In fact, they most likely will not be able to synthesize the many disparate parts of the program when they need to without their journal writing. Without using a journal during complex programs, it is highly likely that learning retention during and after the program will be lower than it should be. Typically, this happens when programs are intellectually or emotionally challenging or have many elements. These can be shorter programs or complex, multiday courses with numerous modules and program elements that need to be integrated by the participants to be of full value. These could also be programs where there is a clear expectation that learning will be converted to committed implementation after the program ends.

Consider these eight suggestions on how to ensure that learning journals are vehicles for active learning and postprogram implementation. First, during the program introduction, describe the importance and the expectation of keeping the learning journal up to date throughout the program. For the naturals, the only encouragement they usually need to hear is "This will help you learn effectively and be in a very good position to develop your implementation plan." For those who need a nudge and a rationale or even stronger motivation because they are not naturals at keeping journals, you could suggest this: "Because of the nature of this program, you will likely be unable to pull everything together that you have experienced without regular journal writing. This is especially the case as we move through the program and, most important, as the program ends. This will be a barrier to you as you attempt to write your implementation plan."

Second, provide a journal in the course materials. Third, make the journal attractive and distinctive in its appearance. You could intersperse famous quotations or quotations from former participants at relevant points that track to program themes and concepts.

Fourth, construct the journal so that it is easy to handle. It should not be simply another section in a program binder. It should be easy to take with the participants as they move around and are involved in different individual and group activities.

Fifth, use a combination of blank pages and some predesigned sections for specific types of entries that correspond to designated parts of the program. Do not overstructure the journal. The majority of pages should be blank.

Sixth, periodically refer to the journal and ask for volunteers to share something they have recorded that is not of a confidential nature. This helps to reinforce the use of the learning journal.

Seventh, occasionally provide short periods of time during the program for journal writing, although the default expectation is that people will write in their journal on their own. And eighth, use the journal as the basis for writing the participants' implementation plan.

Crystallizing "Learning Gems" through Learning Debriefs

The 13th active teaching method is crystallizing "learning gems" through learning debriefs. Active teaching and learning delivers some of its greatest dividends when learning debriefs or processing sessions are conducted. The pure gems from the learning experience invariably surface from these learning debrief sessions in one sentence or one paragraph form. Simply stated, learning gems are the most important points that participants take away from their own personal learning experience. In class aggregate form, they represent the most important concepts, personal awareness, and commitments for implementation that the program participants internalize and carry with them from the program.

Leader-teachers can make the *learning gems* term a regular part of their vocabulary. I used to use expressions like "takeaways" and "clear points." However, "learning gems" conveys much more. The term's imagery and clarity have worked for leader-teachers in dozens of locations around the world. Participants usually hear the term once and then it becomes part of the program's vocabulary. By its very nature, the process of facilitating the participants' identification of their learning gems is a very active teaching and learning experience.

These suggestions can be used to help mine the gems of most learning programs:

- Short debriefing or processing sessions should be held at many or most of the transition points in a program. These are usually at the conclusion of a module or lesson and at the end of a day for a program of two or more days.
- Leader-teachers should always facilitate a learning processing session to help the program draw to a close.
- This closing processing session is one of the most important and memorable parts of a program. Keep it simple, and encourage participants to share one or more of their learning gems. These gems could come from one small, but important, part of the program or might be a synthesis of the participants' valuable integrated thinking.
- Use a variety of processing or debriefing methods.
- Consider having participants use Post-it notes to make copies of the learning gems that they record in their journals. These Post-it notes are then placed on a series of flip chart sheets that are taped to the wall. To do this, include many colors of Post-it notepads at each table where participants sit before the program. Set the expectation of posting these notes on the wall charts during the introduction of the program and watch the contributions begin. I have taught or cotaught classes where

several hundred learning gems are posted. With different-colored pads, it is an impressive sight and reinforces the learning that each participant is doing in class.

♦ Follow up on the previous suggestion and have the learning gems on the wall charts typed and circulated back to the participants as a summary of the program.

♦ Some organizations are using classroom wikis during the program. The Post-it note concept could be adapted easily to a wiki application if participants are using their computers during the class.

You can use many processing methods to identify learning gems. Here are a few examples:

♦ Sentence completions such as I learned…, I relearned…, I realized…, I was surprised…, I wonder…, I hope…. I learned these sentence stems from Sidney Simon 40 years ago and have probably used them several thousand times in all parts of the world. They always help learners to crystallize their thinking and sharpen their insights into how to use and apply their new knowledge or self-awareness.

♦ Write and possibly share reflections from one's learning journal.

♦ Place participants in groups of three. Provide five minutes to generate learning gems in the groups. Rotate around the room, and have one gem shared per group at a time. Consider a second rotation around the room.

♦ Use a 10-to-1 countdown: State that 10 gems will be heard aloud. Start with 10 and count down to 1 as the gems are randomly shared by volunteers with others in the class.

♦ Share learning gems in a whip fashion around the room—one sentence per person, without any elaboration. Hear one gem, a personal quotation, from every person in the room.

♦ Use small groups to construct simple mind maps to identify and highlight learning gems. Divide your class into small groups of four to six participants and ask each group to work on separate flip charts. Give the groups five to 10 minutes to produce their own mind maps based on the module or modules that were most recently experienced. Optionally, share key points in the large group.

When well facilitated, individual learning gems represent the pure gold of the active teaching and learning experience.

The Three-Level Program Design Model

The Three-Level Program Design Model is used in different variations in kindergarten through 12th-grade classrooms and in adult business and organizational settings. The model presented here is versatile and applicable for adult learning situations at work. I have developed my own variation of this model over the past 40 years. I learned the principles of this curriculum and program design approach from Sidney Simon, Merrill Harmin, Leland Howe, and Howard Kirschenbaum.

Most modules or individual lessons can be designed by using each, or a combination, of the three elements of the model:

- ◆ Level I: theory/concepts/facts
- ◆ Level II: personal inquiry
- ◆ Level III: professional application.

A case example on the topic of how leadership can affect the success of a business (see the sidebar) is used throughout this section to illustrate how the three-level model works and how it can help leaders to teach effectively. The entire program uses active teaching and learning methods for each lesson and module, which are designed within the framework of the three-level model.

◆ ◆ ◆

How Leadership Can Affect the Success of a Business

Imagine that you are one of two leader-teachers who are going to coteach a half-day module on how leadership can affect the success of a business. This module is part of a week-long, in-residence program for promising and high-potential leaders in your organization. Three leader-teachers and one external expert make up the team of which you are a part that will teach throughout the week. Program participation is based upon approved nominations of those who have been carefully selected during your company's annual CEO talent review. Those who attend this program do so to enrich their understanding of leadership and to further prepare themselves for additional responsibilities. Steps have been taken to ensure that participants understand what is expected of them. All have met with their immediate report-to leader or leaders before the program. They have been coached on why they were selected and what their obligations are throughout the program and, especially, after the program ends. As a result of their participation in the program, attendees are expected to design and successfully implement an action plan that is developed and peer coached during the last day of the program.

The buzz about this program is very positive, and participants want to be invited to the program. Organizationally, to be invited is a positive signal about how one's career is currently viewed. Participants know that they will have considerable prework, and they will work and study hard and long throughout the week. The program is positioned as an intense, internally designed and delivered executive education experience similar to what one would find in a university setting. Participants are notified of their nomination and invited to attend about three months in advance. This allows them to clear their calendars and provides plenty of time to complete their prework assignments.

◆ ◆ ◆

Level I: Theory/Concepts/Facts

Level I, theory/concepts/facts, is the informational content that needs to be communicated, explored, discovered, investigated, deduced, or synthesized in a lesson or broader learning module. It is the essential "what" of a lesson or module. Here are a few examples of the types of questions at this first level of program design:

- ◆ What are the facts, concepts, or theory to be learned?
- ◆ What is the meaning of this information?
- ◆ What are the big ideas and questions, and how does this information fit in?
- ◆ What is the importance or value of the information to the organization or my team? (Depending on how this question is positioned, it could have relevance for Level II, personal inquiry, and Level III, professional application.)

In a traditional lecture, this informational content is typically communicated primarily in a one-way fashion from teacher to student or class participant. But this content can be better encompassed by a process involving 11 steps—including three steps for this stage of the process.

Step 1 involves exploring the theoretical basis of information and knowledge. As part of their prework assignment, each participant is assigned three comprehensive executive book summaries to read on leadership: *Good to Great* by Jim Collins, *Leading Change* by John Kotter, and *Jack Welch on Leadership* by Robert Slater. The complete books are also sent to participants with instructions to use them as reference material, along with the executive book summaries, to complete a prework worksheet. This worksheet will be used to anchor the kickoff session of the leadership module in class.

The worksheet that is sent to the participants with the prework reading material includes 10 questions that help participants to capture the essence of the three books and to begin to look at the similarities and differences in the leadership approaches and philosophies of each.

Step 2 entails understanding the conceptual or larger ideas and notions of information and knowledge. The in-class leadership module begins with a very brief introduction. The class is then divided into six small groups of five to six participants each. These groups are preassigned to encourage cross-boundary and "silo-busting" interactions as well as the development of new relationships among the participants.

The six groups are asked to work separately for 60 minutes. There are three tasks to be completed by each group during their hour of work. The first task is to share and discuss the individual participants' answers to the prework worksheets. This is a form of peer teaching and is intended to strengthen each participant's understanding of the key principles and concepts of the three books.

The second task is to have each group develop a list of three to five principles, concepts, or facts that they believe are most important—the ones that rise above everything else and that should be remembered by the class participants.

The third task is to generate three questions that they would like to ask the leaders who are teaching the class to answer or clarify. This step is designed to further expand and deepen the participants' understanding of the books they have reviewed.

Step 3 includes comprehending the many individual facts that are the building blocks of the broader concepts and theories. In this step, the leader-teachers ask each group to share the three to five most important principles, concepts, and facts. This is done by sharing one of the principles, concepts, or facts per group on a rotating basis until all are presented (there are often duplicates between groups that are not repeated).

Most important, the leader-teachers use this activity to create a series of teaching moments that come to the surface as a result of this lesson design. Teaching moments are high-leverage points for participants' learning. The leaders often will expand on the points that are presented by the participants and ask questions to create deeper understanding and clarity. Selectively, they also share their points of view on leadership topics as the opportunities present themselves.

This part of the module concludes with a 15-minute segment where the participants ask additional questions to expand their factual understanding of the material. The questions can be answered by either the leader-teachers or fellow participants.

At the conclusion of these three steps, each participant should have significantly expanded his or her basic understanding of the importance of leadership in business success through the use of three expert resources, individual reflection, peer discussion and teaching, and the experience of the leaders who are teaching and facilitating this module.

Level II: Personal Inquiry

If the theory/concepts/facts are primarily the "what?" of a lesson or module, personal inquiry is the "so what?" In a typical lesson or module, this is when the learner thinks through the personal meaning of the content in the form of questions such as:

- ◆ What is the importance of this information to me?
- ◆ What is the evidence, and can I believe it?
- ◆ Do I have confidence in this information or these data? Can I support it?
- ◆ Is this information applicable to me at this time?
- ◆ Why should I consider using this information?
- ◆ What use might it have for my team?

Continuing the case example, here is the way Level II, personal inquiry, might be designed beginning with step 4 of the overall module design.

Step 4 (five to 10 minutes): While still organized in the six small groups from the earlier activities, participants are asked to individually reflect and write their response to several questions in their personal learning journal: "Use your current responsibilities and your current development as a leader as the two points of reference for the questions that follow. What two or three concepts or principles from Collins, Welch, and/or Kotter could help you (1) solve a real business problem or challenge? (2) lead your team, function, or business more effectively? (3) further develop as a leader if you adopted them?"

Step 5: The responses are then shared in groups of threes by dividing the current small groups in half (30 minutes, 10 minutes per person).

Step 6: Using a "whip" around the classroom, participants take turns to quickly state an opportunity they see for themselves that is the result of their thinking in steps 4 and 5 above. A "whip" is an information-sharing technique that allows for many participants' ideas to be heard quickly. Each participant can contribute only one sentence—with no elaboration. The whip starts with one person and then moves, in order, to the person sitting next to him or her on either the right or left. It is easy to hear 30 voices on a particular topic in approximately two to three minutes.

Level III: Professional Application

"Now what?" is the fundamental question related to Level III, professional application. This is when the learner determines how and if to apply the content of the lesson or module to his or her professional responsibilities, professional development, and personal career management. The learner explores such questions as:

- How can I apply what I have learned?
- What will I apply and use that will contribute to our or my goals?
- What do I want to act on or implement, and why?
- What is my plan to implement the things I have learned?
- What are the initial steps in my implementation plan?

Step 7: One of the two leader-teachers relates a leadership Teachable Point of View™ in the form of a story of how improvements in her leadership courage helped her and her team accept what Collins calls "facing the brutal facts." By doing so, she led her business to a record of outstanding performance over a 30-month period of time. She titled her point of view "From the Pits to the Peaks." Her story title and point of view were a rallying cry for the remainder of the module.

Step 8: Participants are asked to develop a preliminary working draft of a plan to implement the one or two insights about their leadership. This plan should state what can make the greatest difference for

- solving an actual business problem or addressing a business challenge
- strengthening their personal leadership effectiveness and personal leadership development (25 minutes).

Step 9: Paired with one other participant, share the preliminary implementation plan and peer coach each other's plans (40 minutes total, 20 minutes to peer coach each plan).

Step 10: Coach the implementation plans (60 to 75 minutes). The two leader-teachers prepare themselves to coach aloud approximately six of the participants' implementation plans. Also:

- Participants are asked to consider sharing their draft implementation plans aloud.
- Five or six volunteers are selected. One at a time, participants succinctly describe their implementation plan (two- to three-minute summary of plan).

- One plan at a time, the two leader-teachers listen to the plans, coach by asking clarifying questions, comment on areas they see as strong, and make suggestions for strengthening (maximum, five minutes per plan).

- During the next step in this cycle, participants are invited to comment on the plan that is being presented if they have a suggestion to further strengthen it (two minutes).

Step 11: Each remaining participant is then asked to share the primary objective of his or her plan aloud. This is done in random fashion but is limited to one or two sentences per participant. An "I pass" option is available to participants who do not wish to share their objective. This usually only occurs for reasons of confidentiality. The purpose of this is for all participants and faculty to benefit by knowing how different participants plan to apply their understanding of how leadership can affect business success.

In this case example, the module on how leadership can affect the success of a business was designed in a linear fashion, with the progression moving logically from Level I to Level II to Level III. Prework was assigned. More than a dozen active teaching and learning methods were used. The module lasted approximately four and a half hours. Most important, the conditions for powerful learning and follow-up are in place. In designs like this, the probabilities of learning retention and measurable impact through implementation are high.

The Impact of Using the Model

Many creative program designs might start at either the theory/concept/facts level, move to the personal inquiry domain, and possibly conclude dealing with application questions and challenges, as in this leadership case example. However, many lessons, modules, or entire programs that spark learners' interest work in and out of these three levels. They do not necessarily progress in a linear fashion beginning with Level I and concluding with Level III. A design could start at any of the three levels. Some designs actually start with questions and challenges in the area of professional application to grab participants' attention and to build a need to know and learn. Some lesson and module designs move in and out of different levels multiple times. This often keeps the participants' attention, involvement, and learning at high levels.

A principal benefit is that when lessons are designed to strongly activate learner involvement and inquiry, the job of leader-teachers is made easier and highly rewarding. Program designs make a very big difference in the teaching success of leaders and the active learning of program participants.

Teaching and learning designs that utilize the three-level model are able to take advantage of the many advances that have been made in the field of active learning over the past several decades. The three-level model, when combined with active teaching and learning methods, can be one of the keys to success when implementing a leaders-as-teachers process in your organization. The program content becomes easier, and often more enjoyable, to teach. The learners tend to be highly engaged. As a result, the conditions for learning retention and application of learning are established. In classes like this, learning impact at a personal and organizational level will likely be higher with three-level program designs than in traditional, lecture-style, teacher-student interactions.

◆ ◆ ◆

Implementation Activity 1: How Can I Use Active Teaching Methods to Stimulate Active Learning?

This activity is designed to assist you in strengthening an existing module or lesson by integrating additional active teaching methods in the design. Follow these seven steps:

1. Select an existing module or individual lesson in one of your organization's programs that would benefit by actively involving the participants in their own learning.
2. Identify which parts of the module or lesson you wish to strengthen.
3. Select one or more active teaching methods from the baker's dozen (or other active teaching methods you may prefer) and determine how to use it or customize it for the module or lesson you have selected.

4. Write the program design.
5. Try the new active teaching and learning design with a class.
6. Assess the effectiveness of the new design.
7. Adjust the design if necessary.

Implementation Activity 2: How Can I Implement the Three-Level Program Design Model?

This activity is intended to help you design a new learning module or lesson using the three-level model. Follow these seven steps:

1. Identify a new module or lesson that you need to design.
2. Review the principles for (a) the Three-Level Program Design Model and (b) active teaching and active learning.
3. Draft your program design.
4. Let it sit overnight. Edit and refine as necessary.
5. Ask several peers to review and critique the design.
6. Teach the module or lesson.
7. Make adjustments as necessary.

Marine Boot Camp Tight

Answering Nine Key Questions to Ensure Successful Operations

*Organizations don't execute unless the right people,
individually and collectively, focus on the right details
at the right time.*
—Larry Bossidy and Ram Charan

♦ ♦ ♦

What's Inside This Chapter?

The overarching theme of the chapter is to make teaching as easy and administratively hassle free as possible for leader-teachers. This chapter offers some key administrative, operational, and infrastructure processes that support a leaders-as-teachers approach. The chapter is organized around a series of nine key questions and answers. The questions are

♦ How do the governance requirements of the leaders-as-teachers process relate to the success of the approach?
♦ What role do learning professionals play in implementing successful leaders-as-teachers programs?
♦ What are the logistics of the implementation process?
♦ How does reliable and advanced scheduling affect a program's success?

◆ Why is it important to contract with leader-teachers before they begin a teaching assignment?

◆ What factors should you consider when matching instructor teams?

◆ How do program champions assist the leaders-as-teachers approach?

◆ How do you use scorecards, dashboards, and "State of the Union" reports?

◆ How do you manage vendor selection and relationships for program success?

The chapter concludes with an exercise to help you directly apply the major points in this section to your own work setting.

The expression "boot camp" in the chapter title has a direct link to a comment Ed Ludwig, BD's chairman and CEO, made to me in early 2000 after approving implementation of the leader-teacher approach. While commenting on the importance of the efficient day-to-day running of the program and the importance of making very good use of the leaders' time, Ed gave me clear guidance to run a program that is *marine boot camp tight*. This chapter offers suggestions and advice on administrative and operational effectiveness that are designed to be customized and used in many types of organizations.

◆ ◆ ◆

Question 1: How Do the Governance Requirements of the Leaders-as-Teachers Process Relate to the Success of the Approach?

All successful learning functions have a governance structure and operational processes that enable it to achieve strategic alignment and integration with the business of which it is a part. These structures and processes are especially important for organizations that have a strong leaders-as-teachers approach because of the time commitment and cultural engagement involved.

Whatever model a company employs, here are some vital issues that need agreement and support by the organization through the learning governance process:

♦ Mechanisms for aligning and integrating the learning strategy as part of the broader business strategy and goals

♦ Development and approval of the annual and longer-term learning strategy

♦ Commitment on the investment level and how the investment will be funded

♦ Belief in, and commitment to, the leaders-as-teachers philosophy, including the practical realities of what it takes to implement it successfully locally, nationally, and—possibly— globally

♦ Encouragement and recognition of senior leaders to teach and serve as executive role models for the leaders-as-teachers process

♦ Management of the mechanisms needed to evaluate the ongoing progress and impact of learning initiatives

♦ Solutions for problems that impede leadership and associate development

♦ Support of continuous improvement initiatives for the leaders-as-teachers approach and the broader learning function.

Question 2: What Role Do Learning Professionals Play in Implementing Successful Leaders-as-Teachers Programs?

Learning leaders and senior learning professionals have expertise and specialist skills in areas such as applied adult learning theory, leadership development, change leadership, instructional design, instructional technology, process management, and continuous improvement. These capabilities should contribute to the success of the leaders-as-teachers process in these ways:

♦ Establishes, builds support for, and leads the leaders-as-teachers agenda.

- Demonstrates change leadership skills that sustainably embed the leaders-as-teachers approach in the corporate culture.
- Builds the justification for, acquires, and when necessary fights for budgetary support for the leaders-as-teachers approach.
- Personally engages senior leaders to ensure their successful involvement as teachers and as executive sponsors of the approach.
- Creates mechanisms to implement training needs assessments.
- Creates active teaching content using the Three-Level Program Design Model that results in effective active learning experiences.
- Creates easy-to-use teaching and facilitation guides.
- Ensures that there are mechanisms in place to help participants transfer their learning into action and implementation.
- Recruits leaders to teach.
- Trains leaders to teach.
- Establishes appropriate mechanisms to prepare leader-teachers to teach specific programs. This includes one-to-one preparation of senior leaders.
- Coteaches with leaders.
- Coaches and provides feedback to leader-teachers to help them continuously improve their teaching and facilitation.
- Determines the best use of blended methods involving technology and leader-teachers to support organizational learning needs.
- Ensures that recognition is provided for leader-teachers.
- Works with training coordinators to create lean and effective administrative processes that enable leaders to teach in ways that are administratively hassle free.

Question 3: What Are the Logistics of the Implementation Process?

Training coordinators serve as the frontline interface between leader-teachers, learning leaders, and senior learning professionals. Training coordinators also serve as the direct client service contact with program participants. They frequently interact with internal service groups and external vendors to ensure high quality logistics and materials support for the programs to which they are assigned that are taught by leader-teachers. Training coordinators serve multiple roles and their multitasking talents are regularly put to the test. Here are specific examples of their responsibilities:

- Partners with program champions and senior learning professionals to develop program materials and facilitator guides.
- Customizes learning management systems for enterprise and local use. Training coordinators frequently maintain the official training records that are essential for regulatory compliance in many industries.
- Builds and maintains program websites.
- With necessary input, develops enterprise-wide and local training calendars.
- Creates and continuously improves lean and efficient administrative and logistics systems and processes.
- Maintains active rosters of certified leader-teachers and is frequently in the role of confirming the faculty for programs assigned to them.
- Provides comprehensive administrative support so programs can, indeed, be hassle free for leader-teachers.
- May manage program budgets and expenses.
- Ensures that site locations are reserved to match training calendar.
- Supports participants so that the learning experience is of very high quality.

Question 4: How Does Reliable and Advanced Scheduling Affect a Program's Success?

The biggest advantage to scheduling programs well in advance is that leader-teachers are able to manage their schedules and commit to teaching assignments. Executives and others in management and leadership roles have extraordinarily busy schedules, and gaining their commitment is invaluable to setting the core of training calendars. The onsite and offsite facilities in which sessions will be conducted are also frequently reserved, months in advance, for many types of events. When training calendars are available six months at minimum and preferably a year in advance, it makes scheduling faculty and facility assignments much easier.

There are two additional suggestions. First, wait until the annual corporate calendar is published for the upcoming year before finalizing the calendar with onsite and offsite training programs and events. The corporate calendar typically has the dates of major events such as board meetings, executive leadership team meetings, national and international sales meetings, and other types of annual functional meetings and conferences. Deadlines for the submission of everything from strategic business plans to budgets, talent review data, and the like also are part of corporate calendars. By waiting until the corporate calendar is locked down, you can avoid a lot of scheduling and rescheduling because the corporate calendar trumps all other events, meetings, and programs.

Some companies keep training programs scheduled 12 months in advance, while others prefer a shorter time horizon, such as six months. There are advantages and disadvantages to both time frames. The biggest advantage is being able to contract for external facilities when programs will be taught offsite. The biggest disadvantage of a 12-month scheduling approach is that the calendars of executives can change quite a bit. And these changes can occur to even corporate calendars that were seemingly set in stone. Changes like these always precipitate a scurry of rescheduling.

The second additional suggestion is to consider scheduling your senior-level leadership development programs up to a year in advance, once the corporate calendar is confirmed, and using a six-month "rolling" schedule for other programs. Rolling scheduling works as follows. After programs have been conducted for two to three months, schedule an additional two or three months of the rolling calendar so that your schedules are always about six months out and are taking into account recent factors that could affect the availability of leader-teachers, participants, budgets, and facilities.

Question 5: Why Is It Important to Contract with Leader-Teachers before They Begin a Teaching Assignment?

Though the leaders-as-teachers process is not secured by a contract in a strict legal sense, it is important for leader-teachers in your organization to feel a sense of commitment and obligation to this process. Few things are as disruptive to the process as losing one or two faculty members shortly before the start of a program to which they have committed months before. My experience is that the vast majority of leaders are very responsible in this regard. Most "red circle" their teaching dates on their calendars and consistently keep their teaching commitments. But every once and a while, someone bails out a day or two before the program is scheduled to start for other than a credible reason. This is one of several important reasons why it is very good practice to have programs taught by pairs or small teams of leader-teachers. Always engage in contingency planning and have a backup plan for staffing programs when something arises unexpectedly.

Question 6: What Factors Should You Consider When Matching Instructor Teams?

There are many factors to consider when matching leader-teachers to cotrain or team teach, including

- Experience levels—matching leaders with more teaching experience and those with less experience.
- Levels of subject matter expertise in various aspects of the program—ensuring that there is solid teaching coverage for all modules in a program.
- Simple availability to teach locally or in a location requiring travel. Steve Sichak, a senior executive at BD with whom I taught on numerous occasions in different regions of the world, regularly arranged business meetings and business reviews that coincided with his teaching in leadership development programs in those areas. This made his availability to teach in these

regions easier to arrange and was much more cost-effective than it otherwise would have been.

♦ When teaching is done in combination with others, it has the potential to be a developmental experience for the teachers as well as the participants. Most leaders believe that they learn as much as the students when they teach.

Question 7: How Do Program Champions Assist the Leaders-as-Teachers Approach?

Some organizations utilize the role of program champions. This role is a unique opportunity for leaders to contribute to the organization's learning agenda while gaining broader organizational responsibility and perspective than they would otherwise. In addition to the more obvious value that this role adds in terms of leading a program on a global, national, or site level, program champions work closely with training coordinators to support their administrative and logistical efforts for that program. This vital combination helps ensure program excellence at the teaching,

---

Leader's Perspective

Steve Sichak (president, BD Preanalytical Systems) says: Acting as a leader-teacher has reinforced the power of teaching as a leadership tool. As a result of my experience, I am much more likely to approach a business situation with the objective of not only addressing the situation at hand but also now considering it an opportunity to teach those who are involved so they are better prepared to handle similar situations in the future. At the same time, teaching has improved my listening skills, and I am much more likely to seek complete clarification and understanding before acting on something. The power of the course content should not be underestimated. Teaching has increased my understanding of the course materials, and the fact that I am much more facile in the course material has helped me apply it to day-to-day situations. Finally, I am very interested in counseling and mentoring, and teaching allows me to satisfy this deeply embedded life interest, while adding value to the organization. It has been a very rewarding experience, and I feel that I have learned as much from the students as I have been able to teach them.

---

content, and administrative levels. Here are the primary responsibilities of program champions:

- Aligning the program with corporate or business strategy and goals.
- Conducting regular reviews of the program at least once or twice a year to ensure that the current design continues to meet an excellent standard while maintaining optimum strategic alignment.
- Working with training coordinators and senior learning professionals to ensure the quality of the program's content, instructional design, materials, and training aids.
- Cooperating with training coordinators and senior learning professionals to oversee changes in materials, routine communications to trainers, certification, and the quality of all trainers.
- Assessing, with the help of learning professionals, the quality of training performance by leader-teachers and taking steps to ensure that the quality is at high levels.
- Advising leader-teachers in the most effective use of the program and best teaching practices.
- Recruiting and ensuring a highly qualified pipeline of leader-teachers to meet program needs. For example, Carl Merrell, BD's manager for information technology learning, says that "the initial leader-teachers who are recruited for a program ... should be just short of zealots and also have facilitation skills already developed."
- Personally teaching or working with experienced leader-teachers to train the next generation of those who can teach the program for which he or she is responsible.
- Facilitating a program-centered community of practice designed to share best teaching practices and maintain program excellence.
- Providing program-specific, periodic reports, program status updates, scorecards, and dashboards. One variation of this is called the program "State of the Union," a concept devised by Bruce Stanley, a very passionate and highly effective global program

champion at BD who has responsibility for the Developing Your Career in Our Changing World Program and who maintains an active program-centered community of practice. His annual State of the Union report card includes statistics on the courses taught, participants, and active trainers as well as sections on business relevance capturing key contributions to strategy and goals, the status and planned changes in program content, and themes that have emerged from feedback.

Question 8: How Can You Use Scorecards, Dashboards, and "State of the Union" Reports?

As noted above, there are different ways of reporting on program status. This is true on a broader scale as well. Like any learning function, one that utilizes the leaders-as-teachers approach should develop metrics that fit the governance process to which it reports. In turn, these metrics and deliverables can be reported on using a variety of mechanisms that communicate contributions to the business. Whether these are variations of balanced scorecards (like the one developed by Mike Barger, JetBlue's chief learning officer), dashboards, or State of the Union reports is much less important than agreement on the contributions made by the leaders-as-teachers approach and by the broader learning function for which they are accountable.

There is also a very important "softer" measurement or—to better express it—perception of the inherent value of leaders as teachers. Whether your organization has five, 10, dozens, or hundreds of leaders who teach, those individuals get to see the learning process firsthand because they are

---

Leader's Perspective

Karen Graham (global diversity inclusion leader, BD) says: As a program champion, I aid the development of other leader-teachers by sharing various resources for them to continue learning about the subject matter. The sources include articles, books, TV shows, media excerpts, and research reports. I also engage active leaders in dialogues on how to improve the current program, as well as seek their input on the design of future programs.

> **Leader's Perspective**
> Bill Kozy (executive vice president, BD) says: The teacher-student engagement process is a significant opportunity to build trust, create broader relationships outside current roles, and create a constructive exchange of ideas on the company and its direction. The classroom is a different place than the meeting room, and exchanges are lively, fun, and highly energizing.

making it happen. They also get to see the thinking that takes place and get to hear and coach, in class, the action or implementation plans that result from programs that they and other leader-teachers are conducting.

Away from the classroom, when leaders are back in their day-to-day organizational roles, they have the benefit of coaching learners before they begin their classes or technology-enabled learning experiences. They also have the responsibility and opportunity to coach their people after their learning experience. The change in knowledge and performance is often palpable. This positive buzz and perception of value gained is very important and contributes to the achievement of business goals and the positive culture that is part of winning organizations.

Question 9: How Do You Manage Vendor Selection and Relationships for Program Success?

There is one rule that I have consistently used regarding the selection and ongoing relationships with vendors in support of the leaders-as-teachers approach. I would only agree to work with vendors if our organization was able to in-license courseware and the external vendor fully supported the leaders-as-teachers process. This also meant that they would help certify and train leader-teachers in addition to granting the company permission to use their material once a written business contract was in place. Agreements like this are win-win in nature if negotiated well. Some learning suppliers do not wish to work with such arrangements. This is understandable given their particular business model. However, many external vendors become true business partners.

These kinds of partnerships can greatly expand program offerings and significantly add to the professional development of leader-teachers. Working relationships with these external business partners also require careful management. One factor that is especially important is that of maintaining a regular flow of up-to-date materials. It is necessary to carefully balance the advance purchases of courseware to gain a pricing advantage with the possibility of having excess material that could become out of date when a newer version is available. This is even more important when technology-enabled resources are part of the equation. Not only might that resource be supplanted by a later version, but an earlier version might not even be supported by the vendor beyond a certain date.

◆ ◆ ◆

Implementation Activity: How Can I Strengthen Administrative, Operational, and Infrastructure Mechanisms and Processes That Support the Leaders-as-Teachers Approach?

This activity is designed to help you to identify areas of existing strength and opportunities for improvement in the administrative, operational, and infrastructure mechanisms and processes that are designed to support the leaders-as-teachers approach in your organization.

Step 1: Consider how these factors work in your organization:

- ◆ governance of the learning function and the leaders-as-teachers process (if it exists)
- ◆ the role of learning professionals
- ◆ the role of training coordinators
- ◆ effective program logistics
- ◆ advanced and reliable scheduling
- ◆ contracting with leader-teachers to teach
- ◆ carefully matching leaders to coteach or team teach
- ◆ the role of program champions
- ◆ the importance of scorecards, dashboards, and "State of the Union" reports
- ◆ vendor selection and relationships.

Step 2: Using a scale of 1 (lowest) to 10 (highest), place a number next to each factor listed above that represents your assessment of its relative effectiveness in your organization.

Step 3: Identify one or two of the factors that could be strengthened or improved.

Step 4: What steps will you take to improve the one or two factors you identified?

Step 5: By what date will you take the first steps?

Step 6: By what date would you plan to have the improvements in place and operational?

Wrapping Up
and Getting Started

Talk does not cook rice.
—Chinese proverb

*There a lot of things you can try to build to last. And what
we try to do in our work is to come up with ideas that will
last ... ideas that will stand the test of time.*
—Jim Collins

♦ ♦ ♦

What's Inside This Chapter?

This chapter is designed to provide guidance in your implementation of
a leader-teacher program in your organization. In addition to summarizing and synthesizing the key points from each of the preceding chapters, you will find a helpful frequently asked question section that will
serve as your personal guidepost on your implementation journey. The
chapter will also help you consolidate your learning by giving 12 quick
but informative reminders to keep you on track. Finally, you will find an
implementation activity, a 12-month road map to implement a leaders-
as-teachers approach. Use this activity to help you to plan, monitor, and
apply what you have learned throughout the book.

♦ ♦ ♦

Learning—Chapter by Chapter

Chapters 2 through 8 have sought to offer both a strategic and practical implementation guide, covering a wide range of topics, to enable you to move your organization to a leaders-as-teachers process. Let's briefly review what we've covered in each chapter. As you review the chapters, begin to think about which ideas are most important for you and how you might wish to convert them into practice.

Six Strategic Organizational Benefits

Chapter 2 demonstrated how implementing a leaders-as-teachers approach makes business and organizational sense. You learned how a leader-teacher program helps drive business results, promotes learning and development among leaders and improves leadership skills, strengthens culture and encourages communication, drives business results, and reduces costs by leveraging your top leaders' innate teaching abilities.

A Role for Every Leader

In chapter 3, you discovered dozens of ways that leaders can participate in a leader-as-teacher program. The five categories explored there contained more than 50 ways your leaders may teach, coach, design, and contribute to learning and training programs and, more broadly, to organizational learning. The ideas covered a wide range of possibilities, from assisting in identifying learning needs and designing a solution to live classroom or online training, to teaching and coaching activities that drive application and keep leader-teachers engaged in the program.

Why Leaders Will Teach

Chapter 4 answered an important question for any learning professional considering implementing a leaders-as-teachers approach: Will busy leaders really take the time to teach? You learned that the answer was a resounding yes, but also that if you do it right, leaders will request a spot on your leader-teacher roster. You found that successful recruiting begins with an appeal to those altruistic aspects of human nature that naturally support the desire to participate in a leaders-as-teachers program. Most important, you discovered the works of four recognized career, leadership, and organizational development experts: Noel Tichy, Bernard Haldane, and Tim Butler and Jim Waldroop. Each of these experts developed concepts that help to understand motivation and the desire to help, support, coach, and teach others.

Change Defies Gravity

Leading and adjusting to change is hard and few people like change. In fact, as pointed out in chapter 5, "gravitational forces" exist in every organization that resist change of any kind—especially big changes. You learned in this chapter how to overcome the expected resistance to change when proposing and implementing a leaders-as-teachers approach in your organization. This can be done through the use of a change framework and key principles based on the work of two organizational change and business gurus, John Kotter and Jim Collins. Kotter's eight-stage change process along with 10 key concepts adapted from several of Collins's works became your touch points. You even learned how to avoid eight common mistakes that often trip up change initiatives.

Leader-Teachers as Stars of the Show

Every teaching engagement is showtime for leader-teachers. But in many ways, every program is showtime for the students and the organization sponsoring the program. The stakes are high, and failure by any one of the players has an impact on both the program and the overall leaders-as-teachers approach. Chapter 6 explored how to recruit and prepare top-notch leader-teachers and prepare them for successful teaching experiences and a good showing each time out. You were given several overarching principles for success, including matching the right teachers and assignments, ensuring that leader-teachers are well prepared and confident, and the consistent use of active teaching and training methods in program design.

Spark Active Learning Experiences

Both the participant and the teacher must be actively engaged in the learning process. Chapter 7 provided a baker's dozen of design suggestions to ensure that this dynamic is integral to the program design process. The methods included storytelling, Teachable Points of View™, questioning, group discussion, problem solving, case studies and exercises, peer teaching and coaching, the use of technology, mini-lectures, "parking lot" issues, learning journals, and learning debriefs. To support active learning program design, the chapter gave you a three-level framework for designing and organizing most program content.

Making Administration Operating Effectiveness Marine Boot Camp Tight

Even if you have done a good job of selling the program to leader-teachers and they are enthusiastic about participating, malfunctioning administrative and operational components can seriously damage any program. Chapter 8 provided guidance on ensuring that your operating practices and administrative function keep leader-teachers on board. The nine questions and answers should make your program as hassle free as possible for your leader-teachers.

Frequently Asked Questions—and Answers

The success of the BD leaders-as-teachers program has given me the opportunity to travel both nationally and internationally to tell the story of how to introduce and implement a leaders-as-teachers approach in many types of organizations. What follows is a compilation of frequently asked questions answered from the speaker's podium or during postsession discussions, during one-to-one conversations with participants, in response to queries during Webinars, or during onsite benchmarking visits at BD.

Why Should Companies Implement a Leaders-as-Teachers Approach?

The simple answer, as demonstrated in chapter 2 of this book, is that implementing a leaders-as-teachers program makes organization and business sense. Most learning organizations work hard to align and integrate themselves with company strategy and goals. When leaders serve as teachers, an organizational exclamation mark is applied. In these organizations, everybody understands the importance of the connection between business results, teaching, and learning. The leaders-as-teachers approach also helps build an engaged and committed pool of current and future leaders at all levels that possess a set of very useful thinking, problem-solving, communication, and facilitation skills appropriate for the boardroom, departmental, or team-level work.

Leader-teachers are role models for other leaders. They walk the talk, and they set the tone at the top regarding the value of continuous learning, teaching, and coaching. Leader-teachers are highly respected. They are many of the company's most effective leaders, and they are go-to people. They often seem to be the first one in line to solve a problem. Many benefit from their teaching experiences to become well known in the organization. Many careers thrive as a result of this type of experience and exposure, and thus both the leaders and the organization benefit.

Let's consider the story of Judy, a leader whose early career track record and professional profile had caught the attention of a several senior executives in her organization. However, despite a well-earned and hard-earned record of success in her first three management roles, she was not well known in the company—nor did she have significant exposure to several other key executives in the organization. She continued her excellent performance in successive roles over about a five-year period. She found herself attracted to teaching and developing others.

Judy participated in several programs that were taught by senior-level leader-teachers. In one of these programs in particular, light bulbs went on, and her vocational compass pointed her in the right direction. She learned a lot in these programs and, most important, she identified a very positive outlet for her desire to teach and share with others what she had learned up to this point in her career.

The rest, as they say, is history. Judy has become an extremely promising senior executive and an outstanding leader-teacher. Through her last two roles and her teaching in leadership programs, she has developed considerable exposure to the top executives in the company. She has cotaught with a number of these executives and worked under their guidance and coaching in other situations. Today, she is at the top of her game, and her teaching has been one of the main ingredients in her formula for success.

Do Leader-Teachers Always Have to Teach to Serve?

The short answer to this question: Absolutely not. Quite to the contrary, there are dozens of ways to contribute and serve. Some leaders I know prefer not to be on stage but want to contribute in other ways. For example, they can serve very effectively through the use of their expertise during the program design phase. Their subject matter expertise is essential to the leaders-as-teachers approach. They can serve as sponsors and also as program champions. They can talk up the leaders-as-teachers approach and write about the effort in everything from annual reports to departmental communications. In both obvious and subtle ways, they can create positive organizational buzz. Most important, on a day-to-day basis, they coach their teams and team members to be the best that they can be. Participation, in a limited or full way, is up to the individual leader and his or her desired level of participation. Chapter 3 offered a complete listing of participation options.

John is a good case in point. He is willing to teach and when he does, he is very credible. He doesn't love to teach but likes it enough that he will offer to teach in his area of expertise two or three times per year. He is a financial wiz and, most recently, he has served as the controller for one of the company's businesses. His most important contribution to the leader-teachers process is as a subject matter expert in the financial arena and several broader areas where business acumen is essential. Actually, what he loves doing is being part of program design teams where concepts develop into active teaching and learning programs. He actually gets more joy watching others teach these programs that he has helped to build than when he teaches them himself. Every one can contribute to the leader-teacher process, each in his or her own particular way.

Do Leaders Really Have Time to Teach, Much Less the Desire to Teach?

This is a question that I hear much of the time. It is a very important one. It really has at least four answers, and the most important one is that essentially all effective leaders teach and coach as a way of doing business. They teach and coach on a daily basis, even though it may or may not be in the classroom. If you ask anyone about the best leaders they ever worked for, their teaching, coaching, and people development orientation almost always will be cited as one of the top five characteristics.

A second answer relates to the busy schedules that most leaders have. When organizations integrate teaching into the fabric of their culture, leaders miraculously find time to teach and coteach in programs and courses because "that is how we do things around here." A third answer is that some leaders simply are not wired to teach in a formal sense. They will make their business contributions in other ways and should be encouraged and applauded for doing so.

The fourth and last answer recognizes the inherent motivation and deeply embedded life interests of many leaders. They love to teach, and they will always find time to teach, regardless of how busy their schedule is. These individuals energize the leaders-as-teachers process, and they spread their enthusiasm to others. Their spirit for teaching is contagious. To understand how these leaders are the heart and soul of the leaders-as-teachers approach, begin by reviewing the principles and recommendations derived from the work of Tichy, Haldane, and Butler and Waldroop described in chapter 4. These principles are invaluable sources of teaching energy and motivation for a significant number of professionals and leaders in your organization. They are powerful role models for others.

Leader's Perspective

Steve Sichak (president, BD Preanalytical Systems) says: The leader-as-teacher approach has helped improve the performance of my organization in a couple of ways. First, the course content has provided the organization with new skills and capabilities. As a teacher, I have become very familiar with the material, and as a result more likely to apply it routinely to business situations. The number of associates who are also familiar with the material as a result of the courses makes it much easier to apply the material to business situations. Next, it has helped develop several staff members. In one situation, the experience of teaching helped one of my direct reports learn that he could have a much greater impact on the organization by modifying his style to be less directive, making him a much stronger leader. Finally, as a leader-teacher, I have been able to make a direct impact on how we do things in the business, not just what we do, improving our overall performance.

Let's take this fourth answer a step further. Try this in your organization. Start with recruiting one or two leaders, preferably senior leaders who are known as having an interest and a successful reputation in developing their people. If at all possible, it would be best if you can get your CEO to lead the way. Some track record of people development is an important clue and a possible predictor of interest in being a leader-teacher. Talk with each of these leaders about having a role in a particular program. Let these leaders know they would be teaching with you or a member of your learning and development team and that you will take responsibility for helping them to be prepared. Despite how busy they are, if they seem to be receptive, you may be seeing a sign of a deeply embedded life interest and/or a willingness to help others and to share their experience and expertise. Teaching in a highly visible program is an excellent outlet for those leaders with this type of interest and motivational profile. Just as important, they can be your pacesetters and role models in creating the momentum for the leaders-as-teachers approach in your organization.

What Is the First Step You Should Take Toward Implementing a Leaders-as-Teachers Approach?

Begin with a formula for success. It all has to do with selecting the right people, matching these leaders to the right programs, and helping your leader-teachers to be well prepared. Do not try to recruit many leaders at first. If at all possible, start with your CEO, because he or she is the ultimate role model in any organization. One or two senior leaders or a senior leader and a highly influential leader who serves in a different role can also be excellent starting points.

The selection of your initial leader-teachers is very important. Their success and their influence with others are likely to stimulate interest in teaching from those who are naturally inclined to do so. These early role models will make a big difference. Choose them wisely. Help them prepare well. Help them to have successful experiences teaching and then watch the energy begin to form in the organization. Recruiting the next leader-teachers or waves of leader-teachers is almost always easier than finding those who preceded them.

Start with one program with the one or two leader-teachers whom you have carefully selected and prepared for success in the classroom. It is especially important to prepare and match the course content with the leader's background. Have the leader-teacher teach in his or her areas of comfort, experience, and expertise. It is often best to have leader-teachers coteach with one or several other leaders.

On a larger scale, build momentum for the leaders-as-teachers process by utilizing a proven change leadership process. At BD, the principles of John Kotter's eight-step change leadership process coupled with many of Jim Collins's concepts continue to prove to be very helpful.

It is also important not to become mired in pockets of organizational resistance. Momentum is built through incremental teaching and learning experiences and through programs that are viewed as having business value. It is also built through engaging those parts of the organization that are truly interested in the learning and development of their leaders and associates. This is called going to the light—finding sources of energy for teaching and learning as opposed to sources of resistance. It is the way to build big mo (momentum) from little mo.

How Important Is Program and Curriculum Design to the Success of a Leaders-as-Teachers Approach?

The short answer is: Hugely important. When lessons are designed to strongly activate learner involvement and inquiry, the job of leader-teachers is made easier and highly rewarding. Program designs that actively engage learners make a very big difference in the teaching success of leaders, because when individuals are deeply involved in their learning it becomes a valuable and rewarding experience. The best way to ensure that this happens in your organization is to (1) skillfully and extensively use active teaching methods in your program design and (2) use the Three-Level Program Design Model as the basic architecture for the program.

Chapter 7 presents a detailed description of a four-and-a-half-hour leadership module that uses both active teaching methods and the Three-Level Program Design Model to engage participants with factual and conceptual content and opportunities for personal inquiry and practical application. These are recipes for success that can be used in many organizations.

What Is the Best Approach to Recruit Qualified Leader-Teachers?

Jim Collins says, "First who, then what." Recruiting and selecting the right leaders makes a world of difference between success and possibly not even getting traction for the leaders-as-teachers approach. Having the right leaders makes both the preparation phase and the actual teaching and learning experience much easier. It also greatly increases the probability of success.

I regularly seek input from leader-teachers wherever I find them, and have done so for years. Here is what they tell me makes the biggest difference for them in terms of volunteering or making themselves available to teach. They want to

1. Be encouraged to teach by the organization's culture.
2. Be able to share what they know including their leadership Teachable Points of View™.
3. Add business value and contribute to building individual and organizational capability.
4. Be supported by learning and development professionals in the preparation period in advance of actually teaching.
5. Be confident that they will be successful when they teach.
6. Be able to enjoy themselves and take pride in their contribution— in part because their teaching assignments will be matched with their interests, backgrounds, experience, and capabilities.
7. Control their busy calendars and be comfortable with the total amount of time that is necessary to prepare and to teach.

These seven conditions are the primary ingredients for the successful recruitment, engagement, and retention of leader-teachers. The seven elements are necessary regardless of whether executives are individually recruited for a specific teaching assignment or broader numbers of leaders are encouraged to volunteer to teach in one or more programs.

It is best to have all seven in play at the same time, but you likely could compensate for the lack of one or two on a short-term basis.

These are the key approaches used to recruit leader-teachers:

- Individually, invite key leaders to teach or coteach a specific program.
- Recruit and develop pools of leader-teachers for identified programs.
- Recruit leader-teachers here, there, everywhere—be a creative, unabashed, and active recruiter of leader-teachers.

How Much Preparation Do Leader-Teachers Need to Be Competent in Their New Role?

Whenever I am asked this question, I am reminded of the many athletes with whom I have competed over the years. The best of them are always trained and game ready when they most need to be. They know how to condition themselves and prepare mentally and physically at an intense level, and they also know how to pace themselves. They prepare in ways that allow them to perform at their best; yet this preparation is done in very individualized ways that take into account their needs, time availability, and other professional and personal obligations. The same is true

---

Leader's Perspective

Wendy Witterschein (a key global leader with BD University) describes her leader-teacher recruiting experiences this way: Whenever I facilitate one of our flagship leadership programs, it's rare that there are not several associates who approach me and ask "how can I become a leader-teacher?" And having experienced a program as a learner, they are eager to join the ranks of leader-teachers who help to bring along the next cadre of leaders.... Most of our leader-teachers consider their BD University faculty assignments as a favorite part of their job, and make time for it despite busy schedules and calendar challenges. One of our senior executives, Steve Sichak, tells me and others that he is a better leader for having taught BD University programs. And he has inspired many of his associates to find their passion for teaching. This passion of our leader-teachers often facilitates the ongoing recruitment of other leader-teachers.

of leader-teachers. Here are some ideas that have worked for me and members of our team in helping leaders prepare to teach effectively.

Match leaders to programs and teaching assignments. At a practical level, it makes great sense to take advantage of the knowledge leaders have gained through their years of experience in the roles in which they have served. It is also certainly important to help leaders to take advantage of their academic training. In addition to their work experience and education, adult learning theory suggests that every leader has individual preferences, learning styles, and personal interests. These preferences, learning styles, and interests are very important to consider when recruiting and matching leaders to programs. These factors are also important when helping leaders discover their own teaching preparation style as they ready themselves to teach specific programs.

Leaders teach best when they are confident that they are well prepared to teach effectively. Fortune does shine favorably on those who plan and who are well prepared. Effective preparation breeds confidence, and confidence helps to bring out the best in everyone in just about all situations. Teaching and leader-teachers are no exception. If leaders are well prepared to teach, most leaders will truly look forward to teaching and will carry the day during their sessions.

There are four categories of preparation that serve to strengthen the readiness and confidence of leader-teachers. The first category is program-specific train-the-trainer certification programs. This is one of the most common ways to prepare leaders and professionals to teach individual programs.

Leader's Perspective

Joe Toto (director of leadership development and learning, BD) says: I have always enjoyed the opportunity to prepare leaders in BD for their role in the leadership programs when we are on the faculty together. I am struck by their enthusiasm and accountability to do well. In addition, it is a special kind of working relationship with other leaders in our organization that many other internal learning and development leaders don't always get to experience firsthand in their company.

The second category is developing multipurpose training and facilitation skills. The third is preparing selected leader-teachers to introduce programs, serve as speakers, or form panels for short modules of programs.

The fourth category is preparing leaders to coteach and team teach. This is the preferred method to implement the leaders-as-teachers approach, with these advantages:

- No one leader-teacher feels that success of the program is dependent on him or her alone.
- There is backup if any business or personal emergency arises.
- There is a stronger chance that leaders will be able to teach in their comfort zone from both a content and instructional methodology perspective, than if they taught solo.
- Coteaching and team teaching provide rich opportunities for learning content, leadership Teachable Points of View™, instructional methods, and facilitation skills from other leaders.
- It improves leader-teacher bench strength.
- It is a great way to stretch your comfort zone by taking on less familiar topics or modules and still know that you have one or more colleagues who can help.
- It is a natural setting for peer coaching and exchanging constructive feedback with other leader-teachers.
- It creates superb opportunities to network in your organization and to do talent scouting of other leaders.

It is very important to individually tailor teaching progressions so that each leader can develop his or her teaching abilities at an optimal pace.

Is Certification Necessary to Ensure That Leader-Teachers Are Seen as Qualified to Teach in Their Topic Area?

The short answer is: Yes—the organization where the leader-teacher is going to teach should put some form of oversight and preparation in place before a leader is cleared to teach.

The topic of certification is a complex one. It ranges, at one end of the spectrum, from certifying bodies to practice within a profession—such as medicine, law, accounting, and teaching—to a much lighter and less formal use of the term. For our purposes, it is meant to describe a leader-teacher who is qualified to teach or coteach a specific program. Some programs have very challenging teaching certification requirements. Several examples are complex Six Sigma and project management programs for which exams and supervised teaching may be required to gain various levels of certification. Other programs have less challenging requirements to teach, and the term "certification" is used with a lighter connotation, meaning that a participant has completed a program and a program-specific train-the-trainer process that helps prepare the individual leader to teach.

Let's take a closer look at Six Sigma certification. There are various levels of competency certification—ranging from introductory awareness training to white, green, and black belts to even the master black belt. This is the case at both the user and trainer levels. Certification is made that much more difficult because of the requirements for actual project demonstration and the measurement of results using the Six Sigma methodology.

If We Do Have a Program to "Certify" Our Leader-Teachers, Is it Necessary to Build a Mechanism to "Decertify" or "Recertify" Leaders?

The goal is to have all leaders who teach be successful in the classroom. Some leaders may progress less successfully and more slowly than others. Work with individuals over a reasonable period of time to help them improve. A very small percentage of leaders simply may not prove to be successful teachers. In that case, it may be best to mutually agree to wait six months to a year to develop greater skills and then determine the best course of action. If additional preparation and practice do not help improve teaching performance, it is appropriate to remove the leader from the teaching rotation or to help an individual gracefully step aside.

I am reminded of a situation when a very well-meaning individual was highly motivated to teach but had very real limitations when teaching in front of others. It was actually painful to watch and experience his difficulty teaching and the uncomfortable response of the program participants. We worked with him for over a year and finally concluded that he would not be able to teach significant portions of our programs. This is where the magic of care, candor, and gentle but direct feedback and coaching paid off. Before we had to deliver the bad news, he approached us and said he had concluded that his hopes were larger than his ability and that it would be best if he stepped back from trying to teach. This fine individual still wanted to be involved in the leader-teacher process, and we also desired to keep him engaged. We found that he did have talent working as part of a program design team. He was pleased with the outcome, and so were we.

What Are the Key Elements of a Successful Administrative Function for the Leaders-as-Teachers Approach?

Key administrative, operational, and infrastructure-related mechanisms need to be in place and working at high levels of efficiency to support a leaders-as-teachers process. When these elements are at high levels of efficiency, teaching becomes easier than it would otherwise be and, administratively, as hassle free as possible for leaders. Leaders can avoid being involved in tasks that are unnecessary and can be distracting. Without these distractions, leaders are able to put all their efforts into their preparation and top-notch teaching.

Some of these mechanisms that can make a big difference for helping support leader-teacher effectiveness include

- governance
- the role of learning professionals
- the role of training coordinators
- effective program logistics
- advanced and reliable scheduling
- contracting with leader-teachers to teach
- carefully matching leaders to coteach or team teach
- the role of program champions
- the importance of scorecards, dashboards, and "State of the Union" reports
- vendor selection and relationships.

Twelve Quick Reminders to Keep You on Track

Building a successful leaders-as-teachers program requires that you keep many balls in the air at once. You are not likely to keep every ball aloft all the time, so to help you keep your eyes on some of the most important balls, here are 12 top program reminders to help keep you on track.

First, fully align and integrate your leaders-as-teachers approach with your business's strategy and goals. Make certain that the reasons and benefits for using the leaders-as-teachers approach are clear and embraced in your organization.

Second, involve your CEO and leadership team as leader-teachers. Having your CEO and leadership team be supportive of the approach is important. But it is not enough. Active involvement as leader-teachers by your top leaders is what sets the tone from the top and serves as a role model for others.

Third, keep things simple and provide a wide range of ways that leaders can contribute as teachers. You have dozens of options and ways to involve leaders.

Fourth, understand the reasons why the best and brightest will choose to serve as leader-teachers. Key concepts from the behavioral sciences help to explain why extremely busy leaders will see teaching as part of their role and will actually be attracted to teaching, coaching, and mentoring others. Use creative, persistent, and continuous recruiting methods to ensure that the best and brightest serve as your leader-teachers. Help your current and prospective leader-teachers who show an interest in teaching to understand that they will be able to leverage their experience and strengths while tapping into their deeply embedded life interests as a teacher, facilitator, and coach. These concepts serve as a constant source of energy and motivation for engaged leader-teachers.

Fifth, keep teaching safe and highly satisfying. This is done first through careful and personalized matching of each leader with appropriate content. Then, the use of customized teaching progressions when helping leaders to prepare will add confidence and serve as a safety net. Use a variety of train-the-trainer approaches. Work individually with your most senior leaders to ensure that they are prepared and confident to teach.

Sixth, emphasize the value of teaching as part of your criteria to assess leadership potential. Include teaching as part of your organization's leadership success factors and competency models.

Seventh, remember that gravity never has a bad day. Use a respected change-leadership process (for example, Kotter's eight steps) to help you gain early traction and to build a foundation for long-term sustainability of the leaders-as-teachers approach. Large-scale organizational change rarely succeeds without disciplined efforts and a coherent change process. Remember that just as in physics, in organizations, gravity never has a bad day. It is constant work to overcome the gravitational pull of organizational resistance and the temptation of business as usual.

Eighth, you can't achieve "big mo" (momentum) until you first have "little mo." Worry little about resistance, and focus on those leaders and parts of the organization who want to be involved. Go to the light—the energy sources in the organization. Enough momentum will trump resistance. People like to be part of success and to be where positive things happen. Momentum and involvement beget more momentum and involvement. This is how the flywheel effect begins to form. At some point, this becomes the norm and part of the culture.

Ninth, make teaching valuable, engaging, rewarding, and fun. Celebrate and recognize leader-teachers in formal and informal ways. This might include coteaching with them, personal and verbal statements of thanks, providing leaders-as-teachers shirts and blouses, notes of recognition, and periodic appreciation luncheons with small gifts, such as a cutting-edge books or CDs. Quote your leader-teachers in articles and company profiles. Help them to be stars when they teach.

Tenth, use active teaching and active learning methods that are supported by the Three-Level Program Design Model. This is a key way to engage your teachers and your learners. It is a highly effective way to design programs and to stimulate learning.

Eleventh, design for real-work application and impact. Ensure that a strong link exists between classroom and technology-enabled learning and the resultant real-work application and impact. One's manager should consistently coach and set expectations before attending or participating in a learning experience. There should also be postlearning event coaching and follow-up. It has been demonstrated that this sequence strongly influences learning retention and the application of lessons learned.

Twelfth, use the cost-effective nature of the leaders-as-teachers approach as a way of gaining additional support. This is a great benefit of the leaders-as-teachers approach, and it can be used to build credibility and serve as a positive influence on other internal processes.

◆ ◆ ◆

Implementation Activity: Your 12-Month Road Map— Implementing the Leaders-as-Teachers Approach in Your Organization

This activity is designed to assist you in planning up to three priority goals that will help you to establish or advance the leaders-as-teachers process in your organization. It will also help you to effectively implement, in a disciplined fashion, up to three priority goals that will help you to establish or advance the leaders-as-teachers process over a 12-month period.

Step 1: On the basis of the principles explained in this book and your assessment of the readiness of your organization, identify up to three goals that will help establish or advance the leaders-as-teachers process in your organization. Include the criteria by which each goal will be measured.

Step 2: Use the form below to assist you in planning how you will successfully implement the three goals identified in step 1. Identify milestones, including criteria for measurement in three-month segments.

Step 3: Use the form to carefully monitor your progress throughout the 12-month implementation period.

Step 4: Summarize your progress at the three-, six-, nine-, and 12-month time frames using the criteria by which each goal will be measured and this outline:

Outline of a 12-Month Road Map: Major Steps/ Achievements

List the three goals that you have identified to establish or advance the leaders-as-teachers process in your organization in 12 months, including the criteria by which each will be measured:	Expected progress within three months:	Expected progress within six months:	Expected progress within nine months:
1.			
2.			
3.			

Three-month summary of actual progress:

Six-month summary of actual progress:

Nine-month summary of actual progress:

12-month summary of actual progress:

Content of the BD Leadership Development Program

March 3–5, 200_
Location:_____ Conference Center
Faculty:

DAY 1

TIME	ACTIVITY/TOPIC	PRESENTER/ FACILITATOR
8:30 a.m.	**Module I** **Welcome** **Overview and Objectives** • Introductions • Program objectives/learning approach • Agenda • Theme: Achieving results and building leaders at every level • The implementation plan	
9.00 a.m.	**Module II** **Building a Great Company: Our Company Strategy** • Our strategic direction • Our roles as leaders in achieving our strategic agenda	
10:15 a.m.	**Break**	
10:30 a.m.	**Module III** **Building My Leadership Concept** Exercise: "Larry King interview of you on world-class leaders" (complete as prework) 1. Characteristics 2. How do you embody those characteristics/"Teachable Points of View"? 3. Discuss in small groups • Several additional perspectives on leadership 1. Perspectives and definitions of leadership	

DAY 1 (Continued)

TIME	ACTIVITY/TOPIC	PRESENTER/ FACILITATOR
10:30 a.m.	**Module III (continued)** **Building My Leadership Concept** 2. Exercise: Small group (4s) discussion: Do we need both good leadership and good management? If so, where are they appropriate? 3. Implications for the way you lead 4. Leaders as teachers and coaches • What our company expects of its leaders	
11:30 a.m.	**Module IV** **Leading Change to Drive Business Growth** (Resource: *Leading Change: Why Transformation Efforts Fail* by John Kotter—prework) • Exercise: "Change processes that have succeeded and others that have failed or proved to be disappointing" 1. Groups of 4s and 5s: Discuss change processes that have worked that you have led, been part of, or know about 2. Which stages of Kotter's eight-stage process of creating major change were used? How? What was the effect? Which of the eight classic mistakes were made? • Entire group: Discuss examples of key points from small group discussions • Individually: What are implications for you as a leader?	
12:30 p.m.	**Lunch**	
1:30 p.m.	**Module IV (Continued)** • Statistics about change: success, failure • Forces resistant to organizational change • Openness to change individually, what are the implications for you as a leader • Dealing with ambiguity and uncertainty • Peer coaching	
3:15 p.m.	**Break**	
3:30 p.m.	Introduce tomorrow's case study: "Good to Great" (written by Jim Collins; prework reading)	
4:00 p.m.	**Our Company Strategy, Performance and Leadership Development—Town Meeting Informal Q&A**	
5:30–7:00 p.m.	**Dinner and Break**	
7:00 p.m.	Good to Great Study teams meet to plan approach to applying good to great principles to our company.	Participant teams
Time to be determined by each study team	Conclude Evening Session/Social Time	

DAY 2

TIME	ACTIVITY/TOPIC	PRESENTER/ FACILITATOR
8:30 a.m.	Personalized Review of Day 1	
8:45 a.m.	**Applying Change Leadership and Decision Making Part 2: Case Study: "Good to Great"—Application to Our Company** • Presentations and discussion • Individually, what are the implications for you as a leader?	
10:45 a.m.	**Break**	
11:00 a.m.	**Module V** **Applying Change Leadership and Decision Making** **Part 1: Group Think: The Challenger Disaster—How Well-Intended Decision Making Can Go Awry (video)**	
12:15 p.m.	**Lunch**	
1:15 p.m.	**Module VI** **Developing Myself as a Leader** • Career graph exercise: The key self-development question • The essence of how leaders learn/grow and develop key principles: —The developmental hierarchy —Job challenge profile (prework) —Career sequencing —Time in job —Importance of feedback —How strengths become blind spots —Peer coaching on job challenge profile	
2:45 p.m.	**Break**	
3:00 p.m.	**Developing Myself as a Leader (Continued)** • Debrief of EQ map (prework) —The importance of emotional intelligence in leadership —Implications for my leadership development —The derailment process: Exercise • Break combined with peer coaching on EQ map	
6:00 p.m.	**Dinner**	

DAY 3

TIME	ACTIVITY/TOPIC	PRESENTER/ FACILITATOR
8:30 a.m.	Personalized Review of Day 2 / Preview of Day 3	
8:40 a.m.	**Module VII** **My Role in Developing Leaders at Every Level** • Changing our paradigm: Survival of the fittest to development of the fittest • Review of key development principles • Human resources planning —A guide for assessing leadership potential: potential —Assessment factors —Learning agility: Learning from experience —Becoming a more effective learner —HRP process —Potential definitions/checklist —Talent management framework —Associate development scenarios practices	
10:45 a.m.	**Break**	
11:00 a.m.	**Module VIII** **Job Sculpting: The Art of Retaining Your Best People** **(Resource: _Harvard Business Review_ Article)** • Understanding the power of deeply embedded life interests in the retention and development of leaders • Applying the principles of job sculpting to your leadership role • Sample job sculpting interview	
12:15 p.m.	**Lunch**	
1:15 p.m.	**Module IX** **Implementation Planning** • Preview of afternoon • Individual work on implementation and development plan (includes use of "Leader as Self" worksheets—parts A and B) • Peer coaching	
3:15 p.m.	**Break**	
3:30 p.m.	Share implementation goals in groups	
4:15 p.m.	Plan for Follow-up Day/Program/Evaluations—Group Feedback	
4:30 p.m.	Summary and Close	

References and Sources

BD (Becton, Dickinson and Company). 2007. *2007 Annual Report.* Franklin Lakes, NJ: BD.

Betof, E. Leaders as Teachers. 2004. *T&D* 58, no. 3.

Bingham, T., and P. Galagan. 2004. At C-Level Interview: Ed Ludwig. *T&D* 58, no. 3.

Butler, T., and J. Waldroop. 1999. Job Sculpting: The Art of Retaining Your Best People. *Harvard Business Review* 77, no. 5.

Collins, J. 2002. *Good to Great.* New York: Harper Business.

Collins, J., and J. Porras. 1994. *Built to Last.* New York: Harper Business.

Denning, S. 2004. Telling Tales. *Harvard Business Review,* May.

Guber, P. 2007. The Four Truths of the Story Teller. *Harvard Business Review,* December.

Kotter, J. 1996. *Leading Change.* Boston: Harvard Business School Press.

Kotter, J., and D. Cohen. 2002. *The Heart of Change.* Boston: Harvard Business School Press.

Leeds, D. 2000. *The 7 Powers of Questions.* New York: Perigee.

Marquardt, M. 2005. *Leading with Questions: How Leaders Find the Right Solutions by Knowing What to Ask.* San Francisco: Jossey-Bass.

Reddy, D. 2002. How Storytelling Builds Next-Generation Leaders. *MIT Sloan Management Review,* Summer.

Silberman, M. 1998. *Training the Active Way.* San Francisco: Jossey-Bass.

———. 2005. *101 Ways to Make Training Active.* San Francisco: Pfeiffer.

———. 2006. *Training the Active Way.* San Francisco: Pfeiffer.

Tichy, N. 1997. *The Leadership Engine.* New York: Harper Business.

———. 2002. *The Cycle of Leadership.* New York: Harper Business.

Tichy, N., and E. Cohen. 1998. The Teaching Organization. *T&D* 52, no. 7.

T&D 2007. Those Who Lead, Teach. ASTD Best Award Edition, vol. 61, no. 10.

Additional Resources

Adair, J. 2005. *How to Grow Leaders: The Seven Key Principles of Effective Leadership Development.* London: Kogan Page.

Aldrich, C. 2004. *Simulations and the Future of Learning.* San Francisco: Pfeiffer.

Bennis, W., and J. Goldsmith. 2003. *Learning to Lead.* New York: Basic Books.

Berger, L., and D. Berger., eds. 2004. *The Talent Management Handbook: Creating Organizational Excellence by Identifying, Developing, and Promoting Your Best People.* New York: McGraw-Hill.

Betof, E., and F. Harwood. 1992. *Just Promoted! How to Survive and Thrive in Your First 12 Months as a Manager.* New York: McGraw-Hill.

Biech, E., ed. 2008. *ASTD Handbook for Workplace Learning Professionals.* Alexandria, VA: ASTD Press.

Bingham, T., and P. Galagan. 2007. *A View from the Top.* Alexandria, VA: ASTD Press.

Bingham, T., and T. Jeary. 2007. *Presenting Learning.* Alexandria, VA: ASTD Press.

Brandon, R., and M. Seldman. 2004. *Survival of the Savvy.* New York: Free Press.

Brinkerhoff, R., and A. Apking. 2001. *High Impact Learning.* New York: Basic Books,

Buckingham, M., and C. Coffman. 1999. *First, Break All the Rules.* New York: Simon & Schuster.

Buzan, Tony. 2002. *How to Mind Map.* London: Thorsons.

Byham, W., A. Smith, and M. Paese. 2005. *Grow Your Own Leaders: Acceleration Pools—A New Method of Succession Management.* Pittsburgh: DDI Press.

Cappelli, P. 2008. *Talent on Demand: Managing Talent in an Age of Uncertainty.* Boston: Harvard Business School Press.

Charan, R. 2001. *What the CEO Wants You to Know.* New York: Crown Business.

Charan, R., S. Drotter, and J. Noel. 2001. *The Leadership Pipeline: How to Build the Leadership Powered Company.* San Francisco: John Wiley and Sons.

Citrin, J., and R. Smith. 2003. *The 5 Patterns of Extraordinary Careers.* New York: Crown Business.

Dychtwald, K., T. Erickson, and R. Morison. 2006. *Workforce Crises: How to Beat the Coming Shortage of Skills and Talent.* Boston: Harvard Business School Press.

Elkeles, T., and J. Phillips. 2007. *The Chief Learning Officer.* Burlington, MA: Butterworth-Heinemann.

Ellet, W. 2007. *The Case Study Handbook.* Boston: Harvard Business School Press.

Galford, R., and R.F. Marcusa. 2006. *Your Leadership Legacy.* Boston: Harvard Business School Press.

Gardner, H. 1995. *Leading Minds: An Anatomy of Leadership.* New York: Basic Books,

George, B., A. McClean, and N. Craig. 2008. *Finding Your True North.* San Francisco: Jossey-Bass,

Goldberg, M. 1998. *The Art of the Question.* New York: John Wiley and Sons.

Goldsmith, M. 2007. *What Got You Here Won't Get You There.* New York: Hyperion.

Goldsmith, M., H. Morgan, and A. Ogg. 2004. *Leading Organizational Learning: Harnessing the Power of Knowledge.* San Francisco: John Wiley and Sons.

Greeno, N. 2006. *Corporate Learning Strategies.* Alexandria, VA: ASTD Press.

Harmin, M. 1998. *Strategies to Inspire Active Learning.* White Plains, NY: Inspiring Strategies Institute.

Heifitz, R., and M. Linsky. 2002. *Leadership on the Line: Staying Alive through the Dangers of Leading.* Boston: Harvard Business School Press.

Horton, W. 2002. *Using E-Learning.* Alexandria, VA: ASTD Press.

Jensen, B. 2005. *What Is Your Life's Work?* New York: Harper Business.

Joiner, B., and S. Josephs. 2007. *Leadership Agility.* San Francisco: Jossey-Bass.

Kaiser, R., ed. 2005. *Filling the Leadership Pipeline.* Greensboro, NC: CCL Press.

Kirkpatrick, D., and J. Kirkpatrick. 2006. *Evaluating Training Programs.* San Francisco: Berrett-Koehler.

Klein, M., and R. Napier. 2003. *The Courage to Act.* Palo Alto, CA.: Davies-Black.

Kouzes, J., and B. Posner. 2006. *A Leaders Legacy.* San Francisco: Jossey-Bass.

Knowles, M., E. Holton III, and R. Swanson. 2005. *The Adult Learner.* Burlington, MA: Elsevier.

Leonard, D., and W. Swap. 2005. *Deep Smarts: How to Cultivate and Transfer Enduring Business Wisdom*. Boston: Harvard Business School Press.

Lombardo, M., and R. Eichenger. 2002. *The Leadership Machine*. Minneapolis: Lominger.

————. 2004. *FYI: For Your Improvement*. Minneapolis: Lominger.

Mayo, A., and N. Nohria. 2005. *In Their Time: The Greatest Business Leaders of the Twentieth Century*. Boston: Harvard Business School Press.

McCain, D., and D. Tobey. 2007. *Facilitation Skills Training*. Alexandria, VA: ASTD Press.

McCauley, C., and E. Van Velsor, eds. 2004. *Handbook of Leadership Development*. San Francisco: Jossey-Bass.

McNally, D., and K. Speak. 2002. *Be Your Own Brand*. San Francisco: Berrett-Koehler.

Meir, D. 2000. *The Accelerated Learning Handbook*. New York: McGraw-Hill.

Michaels, E., H. Handfield-Jones, and B, Axelrod. 2001. *The War for Talent*. Boston: Harvard Business School Press.

Nalbantian, H, R. Guzzo, D. Kieffer, and J. Doherty. 2004. *Play to Your Strengths: Managing Your Internal Labor Markets for Lasting Competitive Advantage*. New York: McGraw-Hill.

O'Connor, B., M. Bronner, and C. Delaney. 2007. *Learning at Work: How to Support Individual and Organizational Learning*. Amherst, MA: HRD Press.

Patterson, K., J. Grenny, D. Maxfield, R. McMillan, and A. Switzler. 2008. *Influencer: The Power to Change Anything*. New York: McGraw-Hill.

Phillips, P.P., and J. Phillips. 2007. *The Value of Learning: How Organizations Capture Value and ROI*. San Francisco: John Wiley and Sons.

Rath, T. 2007. *Strengths Finder 2.0*. New York: Gallup Press.

Reitman, A., and C. Williams. 2006. *Career Moves*. Alexandria, VA: ASTD Press.

Rosser, J. 2008. *Playin' to Win*. Garden City, NY.: Morgan-James.

Rossett, A., and L. Schafer. 2007. *Job Aids and Performance Support*. San Francisco: John Wiley and Sons.

Rothwell, W. 2002. *The Workplace Learner: How to Align Training Initiatives with Individual Competencies*. New York: AMACON.

Seagraves, T. 2004. *Quick! Show Me Your Value*. Alexandria, VA: ASTD Press.

Schein, E. 2004. *Organizational Culture and Leadership*. San Francisco: Jossey-Bass.

Slater, R. 2004. *Jack Welch on Leadership*. New York: McGraw-Hill.

Tulgan, B. 2002. *Winning the Talent Wars*. New York: W.W. Norton.

Useem, M. 1998. *The Leadership Moment: Nine True Stories of Triumph and Disaster and Their Lessons for Us All.* New York: Three Rivers Press.

Wagner, R., and J. Harter. 2006. *12 The Elements of Great Managing.* New York: Gallup Press.

Williams, J., and S. Rosenbaum. 2004. *Learning Paths.* San Francisco: Pfeiffer.

Willmore, J. 2004. *Performance Basics.* Alexandria, VA: ASTD Press.

Yearout, S., and G. Miles. 2001. *Growing Leaders.* Alexandria, VA: ASTD Press.

Zenger, J., and J. Folkman. 2002. *The Extraordinary Leader: Turning Good Managers into Great Leaders.* New York: McGraw-Hill.

About the Author

Since the summer of 2007, Ed Betof has been a faculty member at the University of Pennsylvania, where he is the senior fellow and an academic director for the first doctoral program at a major university designed to prepare chief learning officers. He retired at the end of 2007 after 10 years as vice president for talent management and chief learning officer at BD (Becton, Dickinson and Company), a global medical technology company. BD University has been externally cited as one of the outstanding examples in the corporate world of the successful design and implementation of the leaders-as-teachers concept.

Betof previously held senior functional leadership roles at BD, Hoffmann-LaRoche, and the Reliance Insurance Companies. He was senior vice president of Manchester Consulting, where he created a process for coaching newly appointed leaders. He is a faculty member of the Institute for Management Studies and has held adjunct faculty appointments at the Center for Creative Leadership, Pennsylvania State University, and Temple University. He was the lead author of *Just Promoted! How to Survive and Thrive in Your First 12 Months as a Manager* (McGraw-Hill) and has contributed to numerous journals and professional publications. He served a three-year term, from 2004 to 2006, as a member of ASTD's Board of Directors. He chaired the Executive Committee of the Conference Board's Council on Learning, Development, and Organizational Performance from 2006 to 2007. He serves on the Pennsylvania State University Outreach Advisory Board. He received his doctoral degree from Temple University in 1976.

Index

In this index, *f* represents a figure.

About Berrett-Koehler Publishers

Berrett-Koehler is an independent publisher dedicated to an ambitious mission: Creating a World That Works for All.

We believe that to truly create a better world, action is needed at all levels—individual, organizational, and societal. At the individual level, our publications help people align their lives with their values and with their aspirations for a better world. At the organizational level, our publications promote progressive leadership and management practices, socially responsible approaches to business, and humane and effective organizations. At the societal level, our publications advance social and economic justice, shared prosperity, sustainability, and new solutions to national and global issues.

Visit our website

Go to www.bkconnection.com to read exclusive excerpts of new books, get special discounts, see videos of our authors, read their blogs, find out about author appearances and other BK events, browse our complete catalog, and more!

Get the *BK Communiqué,* our free eNewsletter

News about Berrett-Koehler, yes—new book announcements, special offers, author interviews. But also news by Berrett-Koehler authors, employees, and fellow travelers. Tales of the book trade. Links to our favorite websites and videos—informative, amusing, sometimes inexplicable. Trivia questions—win a free book! Letters to the editor. And much more!

See a sample issue: www.bkconnection.com/BKCommunique.

BK Berrett–Koehler Publishers, Inc.
San Francisco. *www.bkconnection.com*